How to Resist Temptation

Francis J. Remler, C.M.

How to Resist Temptation

SOPHIA INSTITUTE PRESS®
Manchester, New Hampshire

How to Resist Temptation was originally published as *Why Am I Tempted?* (Paterson, New Jersey: St. Anthony Guild Press, 1938). This 2001 edition by Sophia Institute Press includes minor revisions to the original text.

Cover design by Carolyn McKinney.

Printed in the United States of America.

Sophia Institute Press
Box 5284, Manchester, NH 03108
1-800-888-9344

www.SophiaInstitute.com

Imprimi potest: T. J. Flavin, C.M., *Provincialis*
Nihil obstat: F. J. Holweck, *Censor Librorum*
Imprimatur: John J. Glennon, Archbishop of St. Louis
St. Louis, July 14, 1938

Library of Congress Cataloging-in-Publication Data

Remler, Francis J. (Francis Joseph), 1874-1962.
How to resist temptation / Francis J. Remler.
p. cm.
Includes bibliographical references.
ISBN 1-928832-39-3 (pbk. : alk. paper)
1. Temptation. 2. Christian life — Catholic authors. I. Remler, Francis J. (Francis Joseph), 1874-1962. Why am I tempted? II. Title.

BT725 .R46 2001
241'.3 — dc21 2001049623

Contents

Editor's note: Except where otherwise noted, the biblical quotations in the following pages are taken from the Douay-Rheims edition of the New and Old Testaments. Where applicable, quotations have been cross-referenced with the differing names and enumeration in the Revised Standard Version, using the following symbol: (RSV =).

How to Resist Temptation

Introduction

One of the most painful ordeals that God-fearing and virtuous souls are made to undergo is that of being tried by temptations. Temptations meet them at every turn and assail them from within and from without.

There is scarcely a day on which they do not experience the full truth of the words penned by St. Paul: "I do not the good that I will [i. e., that I desire to do]; but the evil which I hate, that I do. . . . To will [to do good] is present with me; but to accomplish that which is good I find not. For the good which I will, I do not; but the evil which I will not, that I do. . . . I am delighted with the law of God according to the inward man; but I see another law in my members fighting against the law of my mind, and captivating me in the law of sin that is in my members."[1]

[1] Rom. 7:15, 18-19, 22-23.

From this passage we can see that temptations assail the saint as well as the sinner. No man is exempt from their molestation. They follow us all through life like our very shadow, and they will not cease to trouble us until we have closed our eyes to this world in the hour of death.

Now, the mere fact of being tempted is in itself a heavy cross to those who are resolved to love God to the utmost capacity of their soul and are determined to keep themselves free from the stain of sin. Sometimes they are assailed only at intervals for a short time; then again for long periods and almost continuously; sometimes only with moderate violence; at other times so vehemently and insistently that they seem to be driven to the verge of defeat and surrender. And this cross, heavy as it is in itself, is made still more so by the fact that often, when the conflict is over, they find it impossible to decide whether they have come out of it victorious and are still in the state of grace, or have gone down in defeat, rendered themselves guilty of sin and thus lost the love and friendship of God.

Not only this: two other factors often contribute to increase their disquietude and unhappiness. First, it may happen that because of a lack of proper instruction, they consider it actually sinful to be tempted; and second, they may consider the feelings and sensations that certain temptations, especially those of an impure nature, produce in the body as evidence and proof of willful and deliberate consent to these temptations.

From this it can easily be seen that temptations may become the source of an agonizing martyrdom to those who are poorly instructed in the subject.

And what is often the final outcome of this mistaken idea of the nature of temptations? Nothing less than this: it may lead to failure in the spiritual life. Mistaking their temptations for actual sins, and finding that in spite of their strongest resolutions they cannot keep from being tempted, many lose courage and say, "What is the use of trying any longer? I cannot keep from committing sin, do what I will; I might as well give up." Thus, lack of proper knowledge induces a fatal discouragement and makes them relax their efforts to avoid sin. In the end, they yield easily to temptations and possibly contract the habit of sin, which may prove fatal to their eternal salvation.

Ignorance of the true nature of temptation paralyzes many a soul and exposes it to the imminent danger of eternal punishment, even though it had been destined to do great things for God and reach a high degree of eternal glory in Heaven.

These considerations have prompted the writing of this treatise. It is intended to serve as a guide especially for souls who are tried by the fiery ordeal of temptations, and to point out how these can be turned into the means of greater love of God, increase of grace and merit here and endless glory hereafter.

Chapter One

Understand what temptation is

Before all else, it is essential that we get as clear a notion as possible of the meaning of the word *temptation*.

Temptation is derived from the Latin *tentare*, which means "to try" or "to test." Accordingly, a temptation may be said to be a trying or a testing of the soul for the purpose of ascertaining its attitude toward God and its fidelity in the service it owes to Him.

To a great extent, temptations are to the spiritual life what various tests on machines and materials are to mechanical and building operations. Before a steam boiler is put into operation, its ability to withstand a determined pressure of steam is ascertained by subjecting it to a rigorous test. Before a beam is placed in a building, its carrying strength is determined. And so in hundreds of other cases. The machines and materials are put through stresses designed to show whether they will prove adequate to the demand that will be made on them. By a transfer of meaning, we can say that they are tempted.

This, then, is the meaning of *temptation* — a trial or a test. In the service of God, souls are tested or tried in order that the quality of their love for God and their devotion to Him may become known, and that they may at the same time be given opportunities of winning for themselves large treasures of grace and merit.

Temptations, therefore, are meant to reveal whether the love that a soul claims to have for God is genuine and true, and not mere hollow sham and vain pretense. They are the acid test of the spiritual life. It is well known that there are certain substances that look so much like gold that they are often mistaken for that precious metal by ignorant and inexperienced persons. Many a man has been deceived by the worthless substance commonly known as "fool's gold." To discover whether minerals that look like gold are the genuine metal, an assayer employs special tests. One of these consists in subjecting the substance to the action of strong nitric acid. If the substance is gold, the acid will have no effect on it; if it is not, it will break up and dissolve — an easy way of proving that what was thought to be gold was nothing more than worthless dross.

This has its parallel in the spiritual world. There are many souls parading before men what appears to be solid and genuine virtue. An acid test is needed to reveal the true character of these souls. This is supplied by temptations. The soul that truly loves God will not allow itself to be overcome by them, but will remain firm and immovable in the keeping of His holy law; whereas that which is only a pretender will offer but little resistance, or perhaps none at all.

God causes some temptations and permits others

As commonly understood, a temptation denotes an incitement or allurement to some sin, by either suggestion, the fear of suffering, or the offer of some good or pleasure. It may be external, as by the sight of objects, e.g., books, improper pictures, immodestly dressed persons; or by hearing, e.g., of suggestive or obscene stories, attacks on religion or the Church, detraction, or calumny. Or it may be internal, as when evil thoughts, imaginings, or desires spring up in the mind, or when feelings or sensations of a sensual character arise in the body without our having voluntarily caused them. These and similar causes make an assault on the will to induce it to give its consent to the evil proposed.

In the Sacred Scriptures we find two sets of passages relating to temptations that at first sight seem to contradict each other. One set appears to make God the author of temptations, while the other plainly denies this. Thus we read that "God tempted Abraham,"[2] while we are assured by St. James that "God tempts no man."[3] To reconcile these two seemingly contradictory statements, we must keep in mind that there are two distinct varieties of temptations: those which are known as *temptations of probation* and those which go by the name of *temptations of solicitation*.

By *temptations of probation* we understand all those special trials to which God at times subjects persons, to prove their virtue, to prepare them for some particular work, or to elevate them to a very high degree of holiness, as was the case with Abraham, the Egyptian Joseph, Job, and Tobias in the Old Law; and with St. John the Baptist, St. Joseph, the Blessed Virgin Mary, and countless other saints in the New. Such temptations are

[2] Gen. 22:1.

[3] Cf. James 1:13.

not incitements to sin, but simply what the first meaning of the word implies: a proving or testing of a person's virtue, as of faith, hope, patience, etc. In this sense, it is quite correct to say that God tempts man.

Hence all such evils as sickness, loss of fortune, poverty, enmities, false accusations, persecutions, wars, and other calamities with which people, both the good and the bad, are often visited, can be designated as temptations sent by God, or temptations of probation.

But the case is entirely different when there is question of temptations of solicitation. These are really incitements or allurements to violations of the law of God that come, directly or indirectly, from the Devil. They come from him directly by reason of the superior spiritual powers he possesses and by which he can, to a great extent, work on our imagination and senses and suggest evil to our mind. They come from him indirectly by what Sacred Scripture designates as "the flesh" and "the world," or by what St. John more particularly calls "the lust of the flesh, the lust of the eyes, and the pride of life."[4] Of these means the enemy of our souls makes constant use for the purpose of enticing us to commit sin.

[4] 1 John 2:16 (Confraternity version).

Temptations of this kind must never be attributed to God as their author. They are *permitted* by Him for the testing of our virtue and the promotion of our greater glory in Heaven; but whenever He allows Satan to tempt us, He always sets a limit to his activities. God will never allow a soul to be tempted beyond its strength and power of resistance;[5] at the same time, He infallibly grants all the graces necessary for victory, provided the soul asks for them with humble and fervent prayer and does all in its power to refuse consent to the evil suggested.

The chapters that follow deal with this latter class of temptations, that is, temptations of solicitation, which commonly are the greatest source of difficulty and discouragement to pious souls.

[5] Cf. 1 Cor. 10:13.

Chapter Two

Recognize the elements of temptation

In every temptation we can distinguish three parts or stages: the presentation or suggestion; the delectation or pleasure; and the action of the human will, consisting either in resistance or in consent to the evil presented or suggested. Let us consider each of these three elements in detail.

Element one: the temptation presents itself

The presentation is the first step of the process by which evil of one kind or another is proposed to a person. This may happen in a great variety of ways: by sight, hearing, smell, taste, or touch — in other words, through the avenues of the five senses; or by thoughts, fancies, memories, images, wishes, longings, or desires that spring up in the soul, either altogether spontaneously and without our having in any way willingly caused them or by reason of past events whose memory is revived on occasion.

Thus it will often happen that you will see, hear, or recall things that place before your mind images of or desires for what you know to be forbidden and sinful. This may occur, and very often does occur, altogether accidentally and innocently and without any fault whatsoever on your part. It may happen at the most unexpected moments, in the most sacred places, and even during the most sacred actions. Some thought or desire or picture of evil will suddenly pounce upon your soul and persist in trying to engage and hold your attention. Or, without your having done anything to bring it about, you may experience some sensation of a sensual or sexual nature. Or it may happen that these things take place by reason of some action that is necessary, such as study or reading, attending to the necessities of nature or the requirements of cleanliness, applying surgical or medical remedies, and the like.

There is a great variety of ways, then, in which evil may be suggested to your mind, even while you are trying most carefully to avoid everything of a nature to suggest it. And the list of the sins toward which this first element of a temptation may tend is a very long one:

envy, jealousy, unkindness, impatience, anger, spite, hatred, revenge, gluttony, intemperance, ambition, dishonesty, lying, stealing, cheating, cursing, blasphemy, vanity, vainglory, pride, and lastly, impurity and unchastity, indulged in alone or with others.

What is the moral character of the presentation? If these first beginnings of temptation come to you without any fault or willfulness on your part, that is, if you have not of your own accord and without necessity or just cause done something to provoke them, so that they are entirely involuntary, they are *in no way* sinful.

That such unsought-for suggestions of evil come into your life daily, or even many times a day, you know from long experience. You cannot help seeing sights, hearing remarks and conversations, reading things, or having contacts with persons that give rise to this first element of temptation. In consequence of this, you will often feel the first impulses of impatience, anger, or revenge; movements of pride, vanity, or contempt for others; and in particular, you will frequently experience the first leanings and cravings of nature for delights and pleasures of an impure character.

No matter how hard you may try, you will find it impossible to escape these suggestions. To be entirely free from them would mean that you had received a very special grace from Heaven; or that your bodily organs and senses and your spiritual faculties were not normally developed; or that you were not a member of the human family and of the fallen race of Adam.

The distinction between *willful* and *unnecessary* exposure of ourselves to a source of temptation and *unwillful* or *unavoidable* or *necessary* exposure to it must be clearly kept in mind. Every unnecessary, willful contact with what we know or suspect to be for us a source of temptation is sinful in itself, either mortally or venially, according to the gravity of the sin to which the temptation tends. (This will be explained more fully in Chapter 4.)

The presentation or suggestion, then, is the first element of a temptation. If it is not willed by you, it cannot be sinful. You are still wholly free from sin, even though the presentation may be very vivid and may assault you so violently as to fill your mind with all kinds of foul and abominable thoughts and fancies.

Element two: the temptation causes pleasure

The second element of temptation, known as the delectation, is the sensation of pleasure that is caused directly by the presentation. This pleasure is most intimately joined to the presentation — so intimately, in fact, that it is inseparable from it. It is in this matter as it is in the tasting of food. If a piece of sugar comes in contact with your tongue, you will instantly taste its sweetness. You will taste it necessarily, without being able to do anything to hinder the taste. No amount of willpower can keep you from perceiving it. If you did not perceive it, it could only be because your sense of taste was impaired.

The placing of the sugar on the tongue, it may be said, corresponds to the presentation, while the perception of its sweetness corresponds to the delectation. We may carry this illustration still further by explaining how the will plays a decisive part in the matter of sin.

Suppose you had taken a vow never to allow yourself the pleasure of tasting sugar. Now, quite accidentally you taste some, or you are forced to eat some. If your will is set against giving its approval to this, so that the tasting is in spite of your desire, you do not commit sin. If, however, you were to rejoice that you had a chance to enjoy this pleasure once more, although quite accidentally, your will would have given its consent and sin would be the result.

This example should make clear what takes place in every temptation. The very act of presentation carries with it a perception of pleasure or a feeling of delight, and this happens altogether without the fault of him who experiences it, because it happens without the co-operation of his will.

Thus, for example, you accidentally cast your eyes on a picture or object or person, or you read something or hear a remark or a conversation, that causes thoughts or images or desires of an impure nature to spring up in your mind. What is the immediate result? Without your being able to hinder it, no matter how hard you may try, you will feel a delectation or pleasurable sensation of lesser or greater intensity, possibly even to the extent of experiencing a violent arousing of your passions.

Or take this example: You are informed that someone has done you a serious injury. The moment you hear of it, thoughts and desires of resentment and revenge spring up unbidden in your mind. You cannot hinder this, do what you will. At the same time, you begin to taste the proverbial sweetness of revenge, despite the fact that you may be fully resolved to practice perfect forgiveness and love of enemies, as commanded by our divine Savior. And this remembrance of the injury will remain in your mind, and the itch for taking revenge in one way or another will continue to linger with you, for a long time to come.

These examples should suffice to explain what is meant by the delectation, which forms the second stage of a temptation. It is inseparably bound up with the presentation, and you cannot escape it any more than you can escape the presentation.

Now, what is the moral character of this delectation? Are you guilty of sin merely because you *feel* it? No. As in the former case, so also in this: there is no sin, even though the delectation may be so intense that it seems to have overpowered your will and forced it into surrender and approval of the evil suggested to it. What looks like true consent is only apparent consent.

This apparent consent, by which it seems that the guilt of sin had been actually contracted, is often experienced in matters of holy purity and, on this account, may become a source of great uneasiness and anxiety to those who are earnestly striving to avoid sins against this virtue. Such persons should learn to calm themselves by calling to mind what has here been explained about the true nature of these delectations. Let them remember that the mere feeling or perception of them is in itself never sinful, so long as there was not unnecessary or willful exposure, without a good cause, to the occasions that produced them.

Element three: you respond

The third, and decisive, element of a temptation is the action of the will in taking a stand either for or against the evil proposed; that is, in either giving its consent or refusing it. While so far there has been no sin in the temptation, no matter how vivid the suggestion or how enticing and strong the delectation may have been, it is now up to you to make a definite decision by either approving or rejecting the evil suggested to you. This is a necessity from which you cannot escape; you must decide one way or the other. You are not free to avoid making a decision.

- *Deciding for the evil.* Let us suppose that you weaken in your resistance and decide in favor of the forbidden thing, by giving your approval to it, or being delighted with the delectation you feel, or by willfully fostering the evil thought, fancy, or desire that came to you, or finally, by carrying out in action what is suggested to you by the temptation. What is the result in this case? The instant your will gives its approval or consent — and not before — you contract the guilt of sin.

This brings us to a point that many people are in the habit of overlooking completely: All sin, no matter what its name, is committed *interiorly* by the mind and the will, or "in the heart," as the common expression is, independently of any outward action or deed. An outward action is not necessary for the contracting of the guilt of sin, any more than such an action is necessary for the gaining of merit. All the conscious interior operations of the soul — that is, all the thoughts, fancies, and desires that a man entertains knowingly and willingly — are so many *acts* before God; and these are either sinful or virtuous accordingly as they are either contrary to, or in keeping with, the law of God. The essence of a sin, therefore, consists, not in an outward bad action, but in the deliberate adherence of the will to what is recognized as forbidden by the divine law.

This very important truth is taught with great emphasis by our divine Savior. "You have heard that it was said to them of old: Thou shalt not commit adultery. But I say to you, that everyone that shall look on a woman to *lust* after her, hath already committed adultery with her in his heart."[6] "The things which come out from a man, they defile a man. For from *within*, *out of the heart* of men, proceed evil thoughts, adulteries, fornications, murders, thefts, covetousness, wickedness, deceit, lasciviousness, an evil eye, blasphemy, pride, foolishness. All these evil things come from within and defile a man."[7]

Thus, if you were to muse knowingly and willfully on some unchaste representation, or paint in your imagination pictures of some impure deed or scene, or entertain the desire to carry out some forbidden action, or devise plans for being revenged on one who has injured you, and the like, you would thereby contract the guilt of sin before God, even though you did not so much as take a single step or move a finger to carry out in deed what you had pictured in your mind. You may not

[6] Matt. 5:27-28 (emphasis added).

[7] Mark 7:20-23 (emphasis added).

have spoken a word to reveal your thoughts, nor made a gesture to betray your desires; yet at the very instant your will gave its approval or consent to the evil thought or desire, you rendered yourself guilty of an act of sin "in your heart."

From this it is clear that it is possible for a man to commit countless sins — and very grievous ones at that — all day long in the secret recesses of his heart (as also it is possible to make most perfect acts of virtue), unknown indeed to his fellowmen and unsuspected by them, but clearly known to God, who searches the inmost folds of the heart and before whom no concealment of evil is possible. In His sight, every thought, every fancy of the imagination, every desire that a man conceives consciously, is an *act* either good or bad, according to the relation in which it stands to the divine law and the intention that accompanies it. For each and every such act, an account will be demanded of the soul in its judgment after death.

We must here add that there are certain actions that are said to be *indifferent* as to their moral value, that is, neither good nor bad in themselves. Such are eating, drinking, walking, taking recreation, etc. But although these are neither good nor bad in themselves, they become either good or bad according to the intention with which they are performed. If performed for the glory of God, they become good and meritorious; if done for a sinful purpose, they become sinful and therefore deserving of punishment.

• *Deciding against the evil.* We now come to the other alternative. Instead of allowing the allurements of the presentation and delectation to conquer your will, you cooperate with God's grace and take a firm, resolute stand against them; you refuse to dwell on the evil thought, fancy, or desire and, in particular, to carry out in action what is suggested to you by the temptation. The temptation may remain with you a long while, pictures of the sinful object may dance before your eyes and haunt your imagination with great persistency, the delectation caused by this may annoy you very much, but with the help of God's grace you succeed in keeping your will firmly set against it all. What now becomes of the temptation?

The answer is a very consoling one. A temptation that is resisted, far from doing harm to your soul, becomes the means of *great spiritual gain*. It directly promotes growth in virtue, in the love of God, in grace, and in merit for Heaven. Your firm resistance means nothing less than perfect love of God and fidelity in His service. It means obedience to His holy law. It is a solid and unmistakable proof of true love of Him, far more so than a hundred of the most fervent verbal acts of love could be. Refusing to approve of a sinful thought, or to consent to a forbidden pleasure, or to perform a sinful action, no matter how enticing the temptation may be and how strongly it may press upon the will, is certainly a far more solid proof of genuine love of God than any number of pious affections could be, especially since these are often traceable to mere sentiment and do not stand the test of temptation.

Perhaps you do not understand how this can be. You may admit its possibility when the temptation suggests some outward action, as, for example, a lie, a theft, an injury to an enemy, or an unchaste deed. But how, you may ask, can it hold when there is question of evil thoughts, fancies, or desires, which, as happens only too often, continue to torment persons for a long time, sometimes interruptedly, sometimes continuously and with great vehemence, even though the will is firmly set against them? Nay, it often happens that the more firmly a person is determined not to give in to the temptation, the more violent and troublesome it becomes. How can we remain free from sin under such conditions?

The answer is this: There is no sin committed so long as your will maintains its supremacy and does not give its approval. The temptation may last a long time and continue to grow more and more insistent; your lower nature may feel a strong craving for the enjoyment of the pleasure offered you; a violent conflict may be raging and robbing you of your peace of mind — all this may be going on, and yet your soul may remain perfectly free from the stain of sin. And not only this. When the conflict is over, you will have increased wonderfully in grace and in the love of God, and will have acquired many additional claims to an endless reward in Heaven.

> This is one of the reasons St. James writes, "Blessed is the man that endureth temptation; for when he hath been proved, he shall receive the crown of life which God hath promised to them that love Him."[8] And in another place he has these words: "Brethren, count it all joy when you fall into diverse temptations; knowing that the trying of your faith worketh patience, and patience hath a perfect work, that you may be perfect and entire, failing in nothing."[9]

Thus we see that in every temptation, there are three elements or parts: the presentation, the delectation, and the action of the human will. The first two are in themselves never sinful, provided that they are not the result of a cause that has been placed knowingly and willfully and without a just reason or necessity to make it lawful. The third element, the action of the will, is decisive. If the will gives its approval and adheres to the evil suggested, a sin is committed. If it resists and refuses to give its approval, the result is the very opposite: not

[8] James 1:12.
[9] James 1:2-4.

only is there no sin committed, but an act of virtue is performed that carries with it growth in the love of God and increase of heavenly merit.

From this we can see that temptations hold a prominent place in God's plan for bringing about the sanctification of souls and their elevation to the sublimest heights of eternal glory. We shall treat this more fully in the following chapters.

Chapter Three

Be on guard against the causes of temptation

Having explained what temptations consist in, we must now set forth the various causes that produce them. These we find to be very numerous, but for our purpose, it will suffice to reduce them to five: the enmity of Satan, Original Sin, the world and its spirit, our past sins, and certain physical causes.

Satan tempts you to sin

Without the knowledge that our holy Faith gives us of God's plan of creation and of man's destiny, both in this life and in the next, we could never hope to arrive at a correct understanding of the origin and sources of temptation, or of the existence of evil in general. Faith alone offers us a satisfactory explanation of this problem.

It is a teaching of the Catholic Faith that the various temptations with which we are assailed are traceable, either directly or indirectly, to the malice and hatred that Satan bears to the human race as a whole, and to every human being individually. Not that he is the immediate author of every temptation — for a great many come from other sources — but inasmuch as he was the first cause of man's fall from the state of original holiness and perfection, he must be considered as the indirect cause of them all.

To arrive at a correct understanding of this important truth of Christian teaching, the reader must keep in mind the following points of Revelation:

Satan, known by the name of Lucifer ("Bearer of Light"), is a fallen angel. Before his fall, he held one of the highest ranks in the angelic creation. As an angel, he was endowed with many gifts and qualities of great excellence, which raised his nature high above the nature of man. Among these gifts were vast intelligence, comprehensive understanding, an extensive knowledge of the laws and phenomena of nature, and great physical power. These endowments, which he received in his creation, he retained in his fall, since they are proper to him as an angelic being, just as reason and free will are proper to man as a human being. Being an essential part of his nature, we say that they are *natural* to him. They are not supernatural gifts, as is the gift of sanctifying grace. Hence, Satan did not lose these natural gifts when he fell, any more than a man loses his natural gifts when he sins. What Satan did lose in his fall were the supernatural gifts of sanctifying grace and the right and title to the glory of Heaven, as Adam and Eve lost theirs when they committed their first sin.

What has here been said of Lucifer applies to all the rest of the fallen angels, the number of whom is known to be very great. All of these, known as devils, are now working under the direction of their chief for the ruin and eternal perdition of human souls.

Accordingly, Satan — and for that matter, the very least of the devils — knows immeasurably more about the things of the natural order, about the universe and the laws that govern it, and about the whole realm of natural sciences than all the scientists of the world can hope to discover in a million years. In the same way, he knows vastly more about the mysterious nature of man, about his soul and body and the intimate interrelation between them, about his passions and inclinations, his talents and abilities, his inherited tendencies and weaknesses, and his leanings toward certain sins and vices than all our physicians, anatomists, psychologists, and psychoanalysts can ever discover by the most painstaking research. And all this vast knowledge is his not through the slow, laborious process of study, but as part of the equipment he naturally possesses as an angelic being.

In the next place, it must be noted that Satan and all the rest of the fallen angels are filled with the bitterest hatred and malice against every member of the human family. This hatred is continuous and knows no lessening. It has its source in undying envy, due to the fact that men are created to fill in Heaven the places vacated by Satan and his companions. For this reason, they wage a bitter and relentless war on the human race. Their one aim is to rob men of their appointed glory and plunge them into the abyss of Hell. In the words of St. Peter, they are continually going about like roaring lions seeking whom they may devour.[10]

But although Satan bears this irreconcilable hatred toward men and is seeking to bring about their eternal damnation, he has only one means at his command by which he can do this. That is *mortal sin.* By no other means and in no other way can he drag a soul into Hell.

[10] 1 Pet. 5:8.

Only those who subject themselves to his dominion by committing mortal sin, will, like him, be forever tormented with the fire that shall never die, if they pass out of this life without repentance and pardon.

From this it must be clear that Satan will leave nothing untried to make people fall into mortal sin in one way or another, and after that to keep them in it if at all possible. For this purpose he makes use of all kinds of temptations. In a thousand ways he tries to make sin attractive. If he does not succeed at once, he does not give up, but continues his assaults with untiring patience. He never loses courage over failures, but perseveres if need be for months and years, in the meantime using every conceivable trick and artifice in the hope of someday succeeding in breaking his victim's resistance and making him yield to some grievous temptation.

Thus we see how Satan is the first of the causes of our temptations. The infinite wisdom of God permits him to play the role of tempter, for Heaven is to a great extent to be the reward of our victory over temptation and sin. But while these temptations are very numerous and often very severe, we have the consoling assurance that God will never allow us to be tempted beyond our strength to resist; and we have His infallible promise that in answer to humble prayer He will give us what grace we need in order to come out of the conflict victorious and rich in grace and merit.[11]

Original Sin makes you more prone to sin

The second great cause of temptations is found in the havoc wrought in human nature by the loss of what is known as the state of original justice or perfection.

To get a clear idea of the subject, we must briefly consider the grandeur and excellence of the state or condition, in which our first parents, Adam and Eve, were placed in the act of their creation and in which they gloried up to the moment of their first sin. It is all

[11] It is not out of place in this connection to remind you that, in these days of growing unbelief and apostasy from the true Faith, special stress must be laid on the Church's teaching regarding the existence of Satan and his design of bringing about the ruin of souls. Modern godlessness, aided by the teachings of materialistic evolution, denies all this and scoffs at it as a fairytale. That this unbelief gives Satan an immense advantage in his warfare on souls can readily be seen by the thoughtful reader.

the more necessary that we do so, since the prevailing unbelief of the day makes many persons flatly deny and even ridicule what the Catholic Church teaches on this subject.

Materialistic science plays havoc with the truth of man's creation by a special act of the Creator, of his blissful condition in Paradise, of his fall from this high estate by reason of sin, and of the fateful consequences of this sin to the whole human race. In the name of science, atheistic professors and writers are continually dinning into the ears of our young people that man is an animal pure and simple; that the human race has animal ancestry; that man therefore has not an immortal soul, any more than a horse or an oyster has an immortal soul; that there is no free will, and hence no difference between good and evil; that there is no such thing as sin; that there is no life after death, no destiny beyond the grave, no Heaven or Hell.

The truths taught by the Catholic Church regarding the origin and eternal destiny of man are scoffed at as so many idle fables. That this skeptical view of life, when translated into daily conduct, must prove a mighty factor in the decay of morality is as plain as the noonday sun. This decay is active in society at the moment;

and unfortunately the evil is not confined to the non-Catholic world. It is seriously felt even in many Catholic circles, especially among those who have received their education in non-Catholic institutions of learning and those who indulge in the reading of materialistic literature. No wonder we find a growing disregard for time-honored standards of morality and a veritable mania for the enjoyment of animal pleasures, which quite naturally means the multiplication of all sorts of temptations and the courting of them as something perfectly legitimate.

• *Man's original perfection.* Against this brood of deadly religious errors it is necessary to proclaim boldly the following truths:

God created the first pair of human beings directly, and He placed them in a state of most marvelous excellence and perfection. This perfection was threefold. There was, first of all, the perfection of their human nature. This means that merely as human beings they possessed a wonderful completeness of form, beauty, health, and vigor of body and that their souls were endowed with the faculties of understanding, memory, and will in that degree of fullness which was demanded by their nature as perfect human beings.

God was free to leave them in this state (known in theology as the state of pure human nature), *but He did not do so*. He was pleased to raise them freely and gratuitously to a much higher state, known as the state of *supernature*. This elevation was in no way due to Adam and Eve; it was conferred on them freely out of the infinite love and goodness of their Creator. In consequence of this, they received, over and above their natural gifts and endowments, the marvelous gift of sanctifying grace, by which they entered into a most intimate union with God as His children, enriched with a full and complete title to the possession of the endless glory of Heaven. In addition to this, they were endowed with the virtues of faith, hope, and charity, the cardinal and the moral virtues, and the seven gifts and twelve fruits of the Holy Spirit, so that in literal reality they "were created but a little lower than the angels."[12] But this was not all.

[12] Ps. 8:6; Heb. 2:7.

The endowment of supernature carried with it a series of other extraordinary gifts that are called the endowments of preternature. The faculties of their souls, already perfect in the order of nature, received a still greater perfection, so that their intellect was free from error, ignorance, and mistaken knowledge; their memory was free from the defect of forgetfulness; and their will was made strong and vigorous by the indwelling of divine grace. The so-called passions were under the easy control of the intellect, which was greatly enlightened, and of the will, which was greatly strengthened by this grace. As to their bodies, they were exempt from suffering of any kind; no sickness or other affliction was to torment them; and they were not subject to the dreaded ordeal of death. They were created immortal. After having lived here on earth the length of time appointed to them by their Creator, they were to be admitted directly to the bliss of Heaven without being obliged to pass through the gates of death.

This, then, was the threefold perfection with which our first parents began their existence on earth. They enjoyed a natural, supernatural, and preternatural perfection. Wonderful masterpieces of the omnipotent creative power of God — how different from the brutelike beings between simian and human that unbelieving scientists delight to make them, in a fantastic ancestry of amoeba, fish, and ape!

• *Effects of Original Sin.* This triple perfection was intended to be the blissful inheritance of the entire human race — on condition that Adam, as its father and head, merit it for himself and his descendants by an act of obedience. Unfortunately he failed the test; he committed his first sin, in consequence of which he lost these wonderful endowments, for himself and the whole human race.

This first sin, with its natural results, is known by the name of Original Sin. This implies the following: the loss of all the supernatural gifts Adam had received; the loss of all his preternatural gifts; and a serious impairment and weakening of his natural endowments. His intellect became darkened and liable to error, his will weakened and unsteady, and his passions turbulent, disorderly, and prone to every kind of forbidden indulgence.

In this way, it has come about that instead of the glorious perfection of original justice, there was handed down to us the sad heritage of what is known as the fallen state. We are all born into this world in Original Sin, in a state of disinheritance. We are infected with the poison of this sin. In addition to this, we carry through life inherited tendencies toward certain sins, by reason of the vices to which some of our ancestors may have been addicted; so that the life of most of us now is a continual struggle with all kinds of evil inclinations and leanings toward the enjoyment of forbidden and sinful pleasures.

Original Sin is therefore the second of the many causes of the temptations that assail us in life. Our so-called passions — which are not bad in themselves, being part of our nature, just as our senses are — have become rebellious to the law of God and to reason, much like runaway horses when the driver has lost hold of the reins.

Fortunately, however, Divine Goodness has not left us helpless to our fate. He has made provision for our weakness by the institution of the sacraments and has promised to give us all the aid we need, provided we have the humility to apply to Him by means of earnest prayer. "His grace is sufficient for us,"[13] to enable us to gain a victory whenever temptation comes our way.

By reason of Original Sin, "our passions have become like a sick man's appetite, which most desires that which would increase his evil";[14] and hence we must always keep them in due subjection to reason and to the law of God. But this can be done only with the help of God's grace.

The world and its spirit can lure you into sin

In the third place, a prolific source of temptations is what goes by the name of the *world and its spirit*, known as *worldliness*. By this we understand the thoughts, ideas, aspirations, and pursuits of men and women who are guided in their conduct, not by the will and law of God, but by the dictates of human passion. In other words, it denotes the conduct of people who leave God out of their lives. Worldly-minded people set aside or ignore

[13]Cf. 2 Cor. 12:9.

[14]William Shakespeare, *Coriolanus*, Act 1, scene 1.

God's unchanging standards of right and wrong, good and evil, and in their place set up other standards as being more agreeable and easy for sin-loving and pleasure-craving human nature. From this it is plain that a deadly enmity must forever exist between the spirit of the world and the spirit of God; for that which the world loves, recommends, and pursues God condemns as sin, which becomes for many the cause of eternal perdition.

Let us take a few examples to show how the world places itself in direct opposition to God's holy law and thus becomes the source of countless temptations to persons of every class.

There is, in the first place, the worldliness of immodest fashions. How many sins are continually committed by reason of this evil — and by persons who make pretense to the love of God and the practice of virtue! Who can count the number of temptations occasioned by persons who clothe themselves in a manner bound to provoke impure and lustful thoughts in all who happen to see them? What a fearful revelation on this point the day of judgment will bring to light! As the case stands, immodest fashions are for a large number of persons the cause and occasion of countless temptations. Woe to those who are guilty of this form of scandal — of making themselves the cause of temptation and sin to others!

Consider, in the next place, the great mass of dangerous literature, especially books and magazines that either undermine faith by attacks on religion or destroy modesty and purity by their obscene stories and suggestive illustrations. Why is it that so many of the popular magazines are continually displaying highly suggestive pictures of women improperly attired or in immodest poses? Why is it that attempts to suppress evil productions of the press or the stage almost invariably meet with protests of "intolerance," "prudery," "interference with the liberty of the press," and the like? We are almost forced to conclude that the producers and vendors of this kind of output have sold themselves outright to Satan to act as his allies in his war on souls.

In this connection, we must remind parents of the serious sin they are guilty of when they allow improper books, papers, and magazines to lie around the house where their children are bound to see and read them. Not only are the children thus subjected to all kinds of evil suggestions and temptations; they are also trained in immodesty and a lack of Christian ideals of morality. They will learn to hold immoral views and do immoral things without appreciating their sinfulness and their harmful effects. Thus is Christian morality gradually destroyed and replaced by a pagan one. This carelessness on the part of parents amounts to "giving scandal." And "woe to those by whom scandal cometh."[15]

Fourth, there are the innumerable temptations occasioned by the motion picture. How this truly wonderful invention has been prostituted to the diabolical work of corrupting the minds and hearts of our children and youths even before they are able to appreciate the difference between right and wrong! It is impossible to imagine a more destructive engine for the wholesale ruin of the innocence of childhood and youth than the salacious and suggestive movie, with its constantly recurring sex appeal. Yet such films are produced by the thousands and exhibited all over the world, so that day after day millions of persons, both young and old, feast their eyes and hearts on scenes that suggest actions of which St. Paul says that they should not be so much as named among Christians.[16] Considering how weak human nature is and how viciously inclined to impure

[15]Cf. Matt. 18:7.

[16]Cf. Eph. 5:12.

delights, such exhibitions are bound to be the cause not merely of many violent temptations, but also of countless sins against the virtue of purity. What a belated frost is to an orchard in full bloom, the salacious movie is to the innocence and purity of childhood and youth.

A few more examples of the workings of the spirit of the world as a source of temptation must be mentioned. There is the spirit of rebellion in modern marriage against the order instituted by the Creator for the continuation of the human race, which goes by the names of race-suicide and birth control; the widespread disregard for the sacredness of marriage; the evil of divorce and consequent adulterous marriages; the growing advocacy of free love, trial marriage, and companionate marriage; the plea for unrestricted freedom of "self-expression," which simply means the unrestrained enjoyment of sexual pleasures and the abolition of the Sixth and Ninth Commandments of God; the almost general practice among our young people — often mere boys and girls — of sinful company-keeping and lust-provoking familiarities; and in general, the gradual abolition and demolition of Christian standards of morality through the unceasing efforts of those who, by word and writing, are working for the destruction of Christianity and the return of paganism, with its unrestricted freedom to enjoy whatever ministers to the gratification of sensual and animal pleasure.

In view of these conditions, it cannot be a cause of wonderment that our blessed Savior pronounces such a withering curse against the world and its spirit, for it is ceaselessly promoting the reign of sin in the souls of men, thus neutralizing His painful efforts to save them from eternal perdition. No wonder He refused to pray for it.[17] No wonder the Holy Spirit tells us that everyone who lives on terms of friendship with the world makes himself by that very fact an enemy of God.[18]

Past sins can be a source of temptation

The fourth source of temptations is found in the sins we may have committed in our past life. This is especially true of sins of impurity. There is in them a peculiar danger not found in others. He who has tasted, although it be but once, the sweet poison of these sins is in many respects in the position of a person who has

[17]Cf. John 17:9.

[18]Cf. James 4:4.

begun to indulge in the use of narcotic drugs. Sins of impurity very easily produce a strong craving for renewed indulgence and, for this reason, often become the source of persistent temptations that may trouble a person for the rest of his life. And even when things do not go so far as this, it nevertheless happens often that the mere remembrance of such sins proves to be the cause of troublesome thoughts, fancies, and desires.

It is for this reason that prudent confessors caution their penitents to avoid as much as possible the recalling of their past sins against purity, for every such recalling, even when it is done with a view to confession, is always fraught with the danger of new temptations. This, too, is one of the reasons experienced confessors will not easily allow their penitents to repeat general confessions, nor even to examine too closely into the sins against the Sixth and Ninth Commandments that may enter into their monthly or weekly confessions.

There are a good many persons who spend a great deal of time in trying to determine whether or not they consented to their temptations, and whether they sinned mortally or only venially. All this is worse than useless; it is positively dangerous. It is useless because they will never be able to fix the dividing line between mortal and venial sin; and it is dangerous because the very act of occupying their minds with these matters is like moving and breathing in an atmosphere full of the bacteria of a highly infectious disease. It serves only to revive in their memory the sins themselves together with the attendant circumstances, to fire their imagination anew, and possibly even to arouse their passion, thus allowing past sins to become a source of very troublesome present temptations.

But what about the proper confession of these temptations and sins? The answer is very simple. When a person has had temptations merely (unwillful on his part) and is certain that he did not consent to them, there is no need whatever of confessing them. There is no rule by which he must make them known. It is good to mention them now and then for the purpose of getting advice or direction; but they must not be construed into sins or confessed as sins.

Second, when a person has doubts about the gravity of the sin he may have committed, the best thing is to abstain altogether from trying to establish the degree of the consent given (it can never be established accurately) and simply to tell the sin as it appears to have been. There are many sins of which no priest, no matter how learned he may be, can determine the exact degree of consent and of guilt. All that can be done in such cases is to tell the sin as it appears to be, to be sorry for it, and to resolve firmly to offer a more determined resistance to the temptation in the future. If this is done, pardon will be obtained whether the sin is mortal or only venial.

Properly instructed persons will not spend much time in the examination of sins of impurity. Without any special searching, they will remember enough about them to confess them clearly and sincerely. And as to sins of their past life that may often come back to their memory and make them fear that they were not confessed properly, let them cultivate the firm hope that, having tried to confess them sincerely, they have obtained full and final pardon from Divine Mercy. And while they must never cease to foster an abiding sorrow for their sins and do penance for them, they must be careful never to call to mind the individual transgressions of which they may have rendered themselves guilty in bygone days.

But the fact remains that, despite all the care they may take to cultivate forgetfulness about their past sins of impurity, the involuntary remembrance of these sins will at times obtrude itself on their memory and imagination, and thus become a source of new temptations to them. This will often mean a long and hard-fought battle. If they are thus harassed, they must above all see to it that they do not get discouraged. They must know that they can turn this troublesome condition to good account. By offering a constant and firm resistance to the allurements of pleasure that the remembrance of their past sins holds out to them, they can do a great deal of penance and make a large amount of satisfaction for the evil deeds of other days.

In this connection we must also mention — for the peace and encouragement of certain timid souls — that temptations caused by sins that have been repented of are no longer willful and therefore in themselves never sinful.

Temptations may have physical causes

We have seen how that wonderful harmony which existed in human nature before the Fall was rudely jarred and disturbed by Original Sin and how, on this account, our spiritual faculties and physical powers suffered a serious impairment. We have also seen how our so-called passions — that is, the inclinations and tendencies of our nature — have become rebellious and are continually urging us to indulge in forbidden pleasures of all kinds.

An equally lamentable havoc was wrought in our physical constitution. Our body and its organs and senses became subject to disorders of all kinds, and in particular very prone to the enjoyment of sensuality, or the pleasures of the flesh. If there were no Original Sin, there would be no disorder in the sexual appetite; but by reason of man's fall from the state of original perfection, the passion of lust has become the master-passion, which exercises a tyrannical sway over the entire human family and destroys its unhappy victims by the millions. So universal is its sway and so great its seductive power that very few souls escape being at least severely wounded by it. Nothing but unremitting vigilance, together with constant self-denial and a firm will, aided by divine grace, can enable us to withstand its onslaughts and resist its manifold allurements.

But what we desire to point out particularly here is the fact that many persons are troubled by temptations of an impure nature largely because there may exist in their bodies certain conditions that more or less directly give rise to feelings and sensations of this kind. It is a rather common occurrence that certain persons, especially among the young, suffer at times veritable agonies of soul on account of temptations of a sexual nature, from which they could in many cases easily be freed, if only they could be taught a few elementary facts about personal hygiene and in particular about the necessary proper care of their sexual organs.

It stands to reason that any disturbance or disorder on, in, or about these organs, such as injuries, inflammation, accumulation of irritating secretions — often the result of ignorance or scrupulosity in the matter of proper cleanliness, etc. — must quite naturally become a source of troublesome sensation and of temptations which, although not in themselves sinful, can easily become an occasion for sinful indulgence. And for the uninstructed, they become besides the source of much mental anxiety and worry, because these sensations are thought to be sinful in themselves.

It is plain that whenever such physical causes exist, ordinary common sense dictates that attention be given to their removal. These are cases in which parents, priests, educators, and physicians must cooperate and, by suitable instruction and advice and, if need be, by medical treatment, help our young people in their struggle for mastery over the passion of impurity and lust. What a wonderful relief from sore distress can often be given by means of a few words of proper instruction to those who are severely tried by temptations arising from purely physical causes! This certainly is nothing less than a form of Christian charity.

Those who suffer from some such physical disturbance that cannot be removed by treatment should not on that account be disheartened. Neither their temptations nor the causes of them are willful and, hence, in any way sinful. These persons do not commit sin by the mere fact that they experience sensations of an impure nature. Let them try to preserve peace and calmness of soul, confident that with the help of divine grace they will remain victorious in the struggle and thus win for themselves the reward promised to the pure and undefiled of heart.

Try to avoid causes of temptation

Thus we see that there are many causes of temptation. Most of them are beyond our control. All we can do is to keep away from them, so far as is possible; and where this cannot be done, we must resolutely struggle against them with a firm will and humble reliance on the never-failing aid of God's grace. By this means, we will be able to pass unscathed through all kinds of unavoidable temptations, even as the three Hebrew youths passed unharmed through the fiery furnace into which they were cast by order of the pagan king.[19] Let us take care never to expose ourselves to temptations without necessity, and God will see to it that we will never be tempted above our strength, but will help us with His all-powerful grace to gain a signal victory over the enemies of our soul.

[19]Cf. Dan. 3:14 ff.

Chapter Four

Distinguish between willful and unwillful temptations

As has been stated repeatedly, there are temptations that come to us without our fault and against our will; these are called *unwillful* or *involuntary*. And there are those which come to us by reason of our having done something that we should have left undone; these are called *willful* or *voluntary*.

Many persons have very wrong ideas about this important subject.

There are, in the first place, a good many who, from want of a proper understanding, mistake their unwillful temptations for actual sins and who, for this reason, live in an almost constant state of disquietude and uneasiness of conscience, which discourages them and in particular keeps them away from Holy Communion at the very time when they need its graces most.

Then there are those who court temptations and invite them by exposing themselves knowingly and willfully, and without any necessity whatsoever, to situations bound to produce them, but who yet imagine or try to persuade themselves that they are guiltless of sin, merely because they refrain from outward sinful actions or because they say to themselves, "I do not intend to commit sin."

As to unwillful temptations, it is plain that very often it is simply impossible to avoid either the temptations themselves or the causes that produce them. To be able to do this, we would have to be deprived of the faculties of our souls and the senses of our bodies. In other words, we would have to cease to be human beings. As we are constituted in this life, we must day after day see sights, hear sounds, and come in close contact with many things that will produce temptations of all kinds: some will affect the mind or imagination only, and others will make themselves felt in the body as well. There is no escape from these, however much we may deplore them and however trying it may be to be always on the defensive against their seductive power.

But it is consoling to remember that these are not necessarily a cause of spiritual loss and ruin. The very contrary is true: they are permitted by an all-wise Providence to serve for the furtherance of our spiritual life, and for the increase of our grace and merit. In this way, they are meant to become the source of immense benefit to our souls, even though they are troublesome and annoying while they last.[20]

But the case is entirely different when there is question of temptations that are willful; that is, temptations that come to us because we have exposed ourselves without necessity or good reason to conditions or situations bound to produce them. In regard to these, many people hold very wrong views, with the result that they may render themselves guilty of serious sins even while trying to persuade themselves that they are merely experiencing temptations that they choose to call unavoidable or necessary.

There are many persons who are very reluctant, and many who are altogether unwilling, to learn the full truth about such willful temptations. Human nature, vitiated as it is by Original Sin, is continually craving for the enjoyment of sensual pleasure and looking for excuses to procure it. Besides, passion has a very insidious way of pleading that we can go halfway at least — that we can indulge in the partial enjoyment of a forbidden pleasure and at the same time escape the guilt of grievous sin.

[20] See Chapter 5.

Hence the unwillingness we often encounter, especially in the young, to learn the whole truth about certain willful occasions of temptations and sins, such as forbidden company-keeping, parties, dances, and movies dangerous to purity.[21]

Certain things and circumstances lead you easily into sin

By *occasions of sin* we understand persons, places, amusements, occupations, and objects that may easily lead us into sin. The same applies to temptations. This definition of the little catechism is simple and clear and requires no comment. It is not necessary that these

[21] It is by no means rare for a retreat-master to encounter protests on the part of young persons when, in retreats or conferences, he explains the sinfulness of promiscuous company-keeping as commonly indulged in even by mere boys and girls. A common argument is "Why are we not allowed to do what everybody else is doing?" This makes it necessary to give a detailed explanation of so important a subject. But in making this explanation, we shall also include occasions of sin, because what is for a person a willful occasion of temptation is often, if not always, also an occasion of sin. Hence, we include both in this explanation.

persons, or places, or amusements, or objects be evil in themselves; it is sufficient that nearness to them, or contact with them, induces us to commit sin, or at least cause us to be tempted thereto. It may happen — and quite often actually does happen — that a person, without any evil design whatever and without any fault on his part, may become the occasion of sin or of temptation to another. The blame, therefore, does not necessarily lie with things or places or persons, but rather with the subject who knowingly comes in contact with these.

Occasions are of two kinds: remote (or far) and proximate (or near). They differ in the degree of facility or ease with which they furnish temptation, and in the quality or nature of such temptation. In remote occasions the danger of sinning is less probable; in proximate occasions, it is more probable. In most cases, however, there is a yielding to the temptation. In theory it is impossible to draw the line between the two kinds and to decide just when an occasion ceases to be remote and becomes proximate, or vice versa; but in practice the thing is easy enough. If you have a well-grounded fear — a fear that is based on experience — that in this or that situation you will commit sin, or at least be tempted, as often as, or nearly as often as, you are placed in it, it is a proximate (near) occasion for you. If, however, you feel, with knowledge and conviction, that you are strong enough to overcome the inevitable temptation that arises from this combination of circumstances, the occasion is only remote.

It is said that danger in moral matters is to a great extent relative. This means that what is only a remote occasion for one person may be a proximate occasion for another, and vice versa. Proneness to evil is not the same in all persons; for all have not the same temperament and the same virtue. Two individuals may take part in a dance or witness a play or a movie; one may be secure from temptation and sin, while the other may be guilty of a large number of sins that are mortal. The dance or the movie may not be bad in itself; it is not bad, in fact, for the one. But it is positively bad for the other and the cause of sin to him; for him it is a near occasion.

Occasions of temptation may be willful or unwillful

The next important distinction is that which pertains to a man's attitude toward occasions of this kind.

Willful and unwillful temptations

We have already spoken of temptations that are entirely willful on the part of those who are tempted, as also of those which are entirely unwillful. These latter either cannot be avoided at all, or they can be avoided only with great difficulty and inconvenience.

Those who are placed in occasions of temptation against their will can always count on receiving from God, in answer to prayer, sufficient grace to enable them to keep from committing sin. But the case is entirely different when there is question of temptations that are unnecessarily and willfully sought, or at least not avoided when they could be avoided. This applies to some extent to remote occasions; it applies with full force to those which are proximate, or near.

Too much stress cannot be laid on the duty of avoiding proximate occasions. The simple fact of willfully embracing or seeking out what a man knows to be for him a near occasion of sin is in itself a sin — either mortal or venial, according to the kind of sin involved — even in the event that *now* and *then* he does not yield to the temptation to which he has exposed himself. There is sin in such rashness, independent of its consequences.

He, therefore, who persists in placing himself in a situation in which he has every facility for sinning, and in which perhaps he often has sinned, commits a sin by the very fact of doing so; and whatever afterward occurs or does not occur does not affect that sin in the least. His sin consists in exposing himself without necessity to the danger of sinning.

The same is true in regard to the reading, by people of a certain spiritual complexion, of certain books, novels, and love stories. As often as they engage in reading of this kind, their minds are filled with all sorts of unholy and unchaste images that enkindle sinful desires and rouse their passions. Such persons render themselves guilty of sin by courting the danger of sin.

The same must be said of certain balls, dances, theaters, and various kinds of parties that in recent years have become such a favorite form of amusement among young people of both sexes. To go to these is usually nothing less than rushing headlong into occasions of sin of a grievous nature. To many of these gatherings the words of St. Paul apply very forcibly: "What is done by them in secret it is a shame even to speak of."[22]

Again, the same is true of the promiscuous and unnecessary company-keeping, which is now practiced so

[22]Eph. 5:12.

extensively, even by our Catholic young people, and kept up indefinitely, even where there is not the remotest idea or possibility of marriage. Considering the weakness of human nature and its strong inclination to impure enjoyment, especially at the time when the passions are developing, it is simply impossible for two young persons to be in close company for any length of time without their being assailed by serious and violent temptations against the holy virtue of purity.

To this list we must add the practice that has become general of boys and girls taking lonely drives by automobile, which offer many and easy opportunities of sinful familiarities and improper conduct. Nor can anything else be said of such liberties as embracing, hugging, petting, necking, kissing, fondling, and other perilous practices of this sort.

The rule is this: When once experience has shown that any of these practices are fraught with the danger of sin, they become sinful in themselves and cannot be indulged in without contempt for the law of God and harm and detriment to one's soul.

At the risk of tiring you by what might seem to be useless repetition, we must here add that there are not a few persons who indulge in a very disastrous form of self-deception in this matter of the willful occasions of temptation and sin. In their fondness for certain sinful pleasures and their unwillingness to forgo them, they try to make a sort of compromise by which they foolishly hope to save themselves from contracting the guilt of sin even while they take the liberty of enjoying what is really sinful.

Thus, for example, they will go to see an indecent and highly suggestive movie and sit through the whole performance feasting their eyes on scenes that provoke all kinds of impure thoughts, desires, and other sins against the Sixth and Ninth Commandments. Or they will take part in a dance during which they find that their passions are kept in a continual state of rebellion. Yet they try to persuade themselves that they are not committing sin, by protesting inwardly that they have no intention of committing sin. What nonsense and folly is this!

In what catechism did they ever learn that a man commits sin only when he has the explicit intention of committing it? They surely must know that a sin is committed every time a person consciously and willfully does something that he knows to be forbidden by the law of God. Having an intention not to commit sin, while doing something that is known to be sinful, does not excuse from sin. On the other hand, if a man were to intend to commit a sin, his sin would be more heinous; it would be a malicious one. But to do wrong and at the same time say to ourselves, "I do not want to consent," or, "I do not want to commit sin" is a disastrous form of self-deception.

Avoid occasions of sin and temptation

This should make it clear that we must avoid all willful near occasions of sin at least as resolutely as we ordinarily avoid occasions of contact with highly contagious diseases. But now someone may object, "What if a man cannot avoid willful near occasions of sin, or cannot remove them? What then?"

If it is a clear case of willful near occasion of sin, the supposition of impossibility is ridiculous. It amounts to saying that sin and offense to God are something necessary. Sin is a deliberate act of the free will; mention necessity in the same breath, and you destroy the notion of sin. There can never be an impossibility of avoiding sin; consequently, there can never be an impossibility of avoiding the willful near occasion of sin.

It may be very hard to avoid a willful near occasion; it may entail a great deal of inconvenience and even of painful suffering; but that is another thing altogether. Whatever difficulty there is, is rather within than without us. It arises from lack of sufficient willpower. But hard or easy, these willful occasions must be avoided or removed. Let the sufferings entailed be ever so great: the right eye must be plucked out and cast away, the right hand or foot must be lopped off, to use our divine Savior's strong figurative language,[23] if the soul can be saved from the evil of sin in no other way. Better by far to do without friends, better to live in a garret, better to freeze and starve, better to lose your very life than to incur the loss of God's grace and be condemned to suffer the endless pains of Hell.

But such extremes are rarely called for. It is small sacrifices that are demanded, for the most part. True, it sometimes seems harder to make these than to make great ones. But a firm determination to avoid Hell and to win Heaven at any cost, and the application of ordinary, everyday self-denial and penance — virtues not much in favor with those who love to court the danger

[23] Cf. Matt. 18:8-9.

of sin — will go a long way toward producing the necessary effect. An ounce of self-denial will work miracles in sluggard, cowardly souls.

Willful occasions and confession

One more point of the greatest importance must be explained in this connection. It is the attitude a person must take toward willful near occasions of sin when he is preparing to receive the sacrament of Penance. Is he sincere in his hatred and detestation of sin, as is required of him if he desires to obtain God's pardon for it? If he is, he must be equally sincere in his hatred and detestation of what he knows leads him into sin. He must be firmly resolved to avoid this, cost what it may, no less than the sin itself.

Unless these are his dispositions, he had better not go to Confession, for he will not obtain forgiveness from God. He will depart unabsolved, having deceived both himself and his confessor. He will leave the church a greater sinner than he entered it. He will be guilty of the sin of sacrilege.

If he states his case honestly — that the dances or the movies he attends, or the dates with a girlfriend, are almost always, if not always, the occasion of grievous sin — he will not receive absolution unless he has seriously promised to avoid this occasion for the future. And if he does not state his case honestly, he is telling a lie to the Holy Spirit, and the more heinous sin of sacrilege fastens itself on his guilty soul. A sincere confession does not consist in a mere routine telling of our sins; it is much more. It is a complete renunciation of sin and of all that leads to sin. It is a hatred of sin. And when a man has a true hatred of anything, he will keep it at a distance and out of sight as much as possible.

Is it not to be feared that many confessions are bad and sacrilegious simply because penitents fail to make the resolution to avoid not only the sins they have to confess, but also what experience has taught them to be willful near occasions of such sins?

There are apparently a good many persons who fail to take a right view of this matter. They seem to imagine that all that is necessary for obtaining forgiveness of their sins is to tell them to a priest, but that they have the right to continue to frequent those situations which are the cause of their sins. Some even have the hardihood to dispute this point with their confessor when he insists on their giving up such willful occasions, as, for instance, sinful company-keeping or dances or movies, when these have repeatedly been the cause to them of mortal sin. "Why should I not have the right to do what everybody else is doing?" is a petulant question sometimes addressed to priests in the tribunal of Penance.

All who take a serious view of the all-important question of their soul's salvation must adopt the same policy in regard to occasions of sin as they are willing to adopt when there is question of avoiding contagion from virulent diseases. They know that the secret of immunity is found in the careful avoidance of contacts with the specific germs of these diseases. Hence, they take every possible precaution against the danger of such contacts. They gladly yield obedience to the rules made by boards of health, even when such obedience means great inconvenience or loss of business and money. So also will good Christians readily comply with the warnings of conscience and the rules of their Church in matters of moral contagion, even though this means much self-denial and the giving up of pleasures for which human nature has a very strong craving. Those who obey are safe from countless sins; those who disobey may have to pay dearly for rashly exposing themselves to what tends by its very nature to the ruin of their souls.

It is of supreme importance, therefore, to avoid resolutely all unnecessary contacts with what we know to be the cause or occasion of sins and temptations. This is a grave duty that every man owes to himself. He cannot afford to lose his immortal soul, for if he loses it, "what exchange shall he give for it?"[24] Sin places him in imminent danger of losing it, and temptation is the gateway to sin. He who willfully invites or courts temptation cannot expect that God will work a miracle to preserve him from falling. "He that loveth the danger shall perish in it."[25] Deliberately to place ourselves within reach of temptation, and then to pray for grace not to consent to evil, is an insult to God and a mockery of His infinite holiness.

Our firm resolution must be to fly from all willful occasions of sin and temptation as from the fangs of a poisonous serpent. "If thou give to thy soul her desires, she will make thee a joy to thy enemies."

[24] Cf. Mark 8:37.

[25] Ecclus. 3:27 (RSV = Sir. 3:26).

Chapter 5

Learn to benefit from temptation

"Why does God allow us to be tempted?" is a question people are often moved to ask with a considerable amount of impatience and doubt of God's justice, just as they often ask the other question: "Why must we suffer?"

Since it is a truth of Catholic Faith that nothing in the affairs of men happens accidentally or by chance, but always according to the will and direction of an all-wise and all-loving Providence, it must also be for a good and useful purpose that we are subjected to the trying ordeal of temptations of every sort.

The benefits we are meant to derive from our temptations have already been indicated. In this chapter we will explain the subject at greater length and show that our temptations are designed to serve: for the probation of the soul, for the growth of humility, as penance for past sins, for the growth of the love of God, and for the growth of our merit here and of our glory hereafter.

How to Resist Temptation

Temptations prove your love for God

It is well known that true patriotism does not consist in saluting our flag, nor in making eloquent speeches about the glory of dying for our country, nor even in boasting in time of peace about our willingness to enlist and march to the front. Any coward can do this. True patriotism manifests itself by prompt obedience to the call to arms when danger threatens, cheerful readiness in bearing the hardships of campaigns, and the braving of shot and shell when the order is given to advance against the enemy's lines.

So, too, is he a hero, in the truest sense of the word, who, having fallen into the hands of the enemy, refuses to become a traitor to his country. Large sums of money or other bribes may be offered him for complying; harsh treatment and perhaps death are threatened him if he refuses. He spurns the former and submits to the latter. He cheerfully endures hunger and thirst and imprisonment, and finally lays down his life, rather than render himself guilty of treason against his native land. Is not such a one just as truly a hero in the eyes of his countrymen as is the soldier who loses his life in the heat of battle?

So is it with a soul that is molested and tormented by temptations. They are designed to be a means of proving and testing its fidelity and loyalty to God. There are heroes in the service of God who become such by shedding their blood in martyrdom, and there are heroes who are made such by their unyielding resistance to the temptations that assail them and entice them. They who oppose a firm determination to the blandishments of sensual delight, no matter how alluring; they who refuse to listen to the promptings of unkindness, uncharitableness, and revenge; they who do not yield so much as an inch to the gratification of some strong passion that is urging them on, pleading with them, almost compelling them to taste a few drops at least of the forbidden pleasure of sin — these are surely as heroic soldiers in the army of God as are those who are called upon to lay down their lives for their Faith.

This should make it clear that commonly the trying ordeal of temptation is permitted by God to prove the quality of the love His servants profess to have for Him. There is not a saint in Heaven who did not have to undergo this probation. Souls destined for Heaven must be tried by the fires of temptation, as gold and silver are tested by the fires of the refining furnace.

Temptations help you grow in humility

This is not the place for explaining the nature and necessity of the distinctively Christian virtue known as humility. You know that without humility it is impossible to please God and persevere in His grace. What we desire to point out here is the influence that temptations have on the growth and perfection of humility.

All men, even those who have made the greatest progress in holiness, are, as long as their earthly life lasts, in danger of losing the grace of God, especially by self-conceit, self-sufficiency, and pride. No man has the promise of absolute security. No man is assured of perseverance to the end. All through life, each must work out his salvation "with fear and trembling."[26] There is danger that, after a long period of success, we may come to attribute it all to our own strength and not to the help and grace of God. There is danger that progress may foster self-complacency and self-sufficiency, leading to the gradual neglect of prayer and a growing tepidity in God's service, after which, a lapse into grievous sin is only a matter of time and opportunity.

[26] Phil. 2:12.

There is another danger to certain persons: that of acquiring the habit of judging harshly their neighbors' actions. Unmindful of the warning "He that thinketh himself to stand, let him take heed lest he fall,"[27] they may become mercilessly severe in condemning the sins and wrongdoings they observe in others. They are thus liable to commit very serious sins against the essential virtue of charity.

Now, it is a matter of common experience that temptations, rightly understood, help us to foster in ourselves sentiments of true humility. They reveal to us our innate weaknesses; they show us to what low and mean and base things our sin-tainted nature inclines us; and they give us to understand that when we are left to our own strength, there is no depth of iniquity and immorality into which we may not be hurled by our passions. Surely this knowledge is calculated to make us cherish humility as a means of escape from the danger of losing our souls through self-conceit and pride.

Even the best and most virtuous men are very much like crippled children who cannot walk unless they are led by the hand of another. Even saints must be held by

[27] 1 Cor. 10:12.

the hand of God. The moment they let go of it, perhaps thinking they need His help no longer, or the moment He stops holding them up, in punishment of their pride or want of charity, they are bound to fall and sustain severe injuries in doing so.

Those who are truly humble will never presume to judge and condemn others, even when they see them committing very serious wrongs. They will say to themselves, "Who knows how much more grievously I would sin if I were exposed to the same temptations as these persons?" or, "Who can tell how much better these persons would be than I am if they had received from God the graces that have been granted to me?"

Temptations are, therefore, a great help in keeping us always mindful of our utter dependence on the grace of God, and of the necessity of fostering at all times sentiments of that humility which is so essential for securing from God the grace of final perseverance.

Through temptations you can atone for past sins

A third benefit to be derived from the ordeal of temptations is the practice of penance and atonement for past sins. When speaking of the causes of temptations, we stated that our past indulgence in forbidden pleasures might easily become the source of lifelong and persistent temptations to renewed indulgence. This is a very painful and trying condition for those who have truly repented and are seeking to lead a virtuous life. But they can console themselves by reflecting that this very state of temptation, troublesome and hard though it is, furnishes excellent opportunities for making atonement and satisfaction to Divine Justice for their evil deeds of earlier years.

The reason for this is plain. Just as fasting — that is, abstaining from the pleasures of the palate by limiting the quantity or quality of our food and drink — is a form of penance that helps greatly to cancel the debt of punishment contracted by sin, so also is the steadfast refusal to yield to the desire of gratifying our passions and again enjoying the delights of forbidden pleasure, a most useful and efficient means of satisfying for our past sinful indulgences. And not only that: this form of penance is in a certain sense even more necessary than abstaining from food and drink.

Take, for example, a man who is firmly resolved to lead a holy and virtuous life after having led one of great sinfulness. His conversion is genuine and sincere. Nevertheless he finds that the memory of his past sinful pleasures often forces itself on his attention, and he is strongly tempted to repeat certain acts in order to experience these pleasures anew. Perhaps the craving for them becomes very violent. His lower nature and his passions plead with him and entreat him to grant them that indulgence just once more. This temptation becomes a heavy cross to him. A fierce struggle is going on between his passions and his will. But with the help of God's grace, he resists manfully and holds his ground. Remembering with grief and sorrow his many past sins, he patiently submits to the hardships of this wearisome warfare and offers them up as partial payment of the debt of punishment that he contracted, by having yielded to these same temptations in the past and polluted his soul with the filth of sin. Is not this a most excellent, as well as a most necessary, form of penance?

It must be borne in mind that penance is done not only by chastising ourselves for sins committed, but also by denying ourselves and refusing to grant to the passions what they crave by the commission of new sins. This latter kind of penance is no less necessary than the former. Thus a man may seek to do penance for his past sins by keeping a rigorous fast on bread and water; but if at the same time he takes no care to resist temptations — for example, the temptation to speak or act unkindly, to omit some of his daily prayers, or to indulge in pastimes and amusements that are for him occasions of sin — he is certainly not practicing a form of penance acceptable to God or beneficial to his soul.

Far more necessary than fasting from food and drink is the practice of perfect patience with his neighbor, the refraining from saying and doing unkind things, fidelity to his prayers and the duties of his state of life, and in the matter of holy purity, the resolute avoidance of every form of dangerous amusement. And all this is for the purpose of proving to God that he is sincerely sorry for his past sinfulness and deeply in earnest about making full satisfaction for all the evil he may have done.

Hence, if you are troubled by temptations that have their roots in some sinful indulgence in your past life, try to convert this condition into a means of penance and atonement. Every act of resistance is an act of true love of God, and therefore possesses the power of canceling a certain amount of the punishment that stands against you and that must be paid off completely before you can be admitted to the enjoyment of the glory of Heaven.

Temptations help you grow in love for God

In the fourth place, temptations are designed to make us grow in the love of God. They furnish the most excellent material for the perfect practice of this virtue. Every resistance to a temptation is equivalent to an act of divine love. And the more violent our temptations are, and the longer they last, the more ample opportunities do they furnish us for exhibiting our love of God in the very highest degree of perfection. Pure and perfect love does not mean that we are to be free from temptations, but that we resolutely set our face against them and refuse to offend God by yielding to them.

What does it mean to be tempted? It means that there comes to us a suggestion, a solicitation, or an enticement to do or enjoy something we know to be displeasing to God. We are asked to disregard His holy will by trampling on one of His commandments; to prefer some passing vile pleasure to His friendship here and the endless glory He has promised hereafter. We are asked to offer an insult to Him. To yield to a temptation, therefore, means that we spurn His love, defy His holy will, insult His supreme majesty, trample underfoot the

Precious Blood of our divine Savior, and crucify the Son of God anew, making a mockery of Him.

And what does it mean to resist temptations? It means that, for the love of God, we despise the sinful pleasures offered us; that we are determined to do God's holy will in all things; that we fear and dread nothing so much as to offend and grieve Him; that we are willing to suffer any kind of pain rather than lose His friendship, love, and grace. Is not this a most solid and incontestable proof of genuine and perfect love of God? It is impossible to think of more convincing proof. And this is all the more true the more violent the temptations are and the longer they continue to assail and torment our souls.

Judge for yourself which is the better and more faithful servant of God: he who has nothing or only a little to endure for Him in the way of temptations, so that his life runs smoothly and placidly; or he who bravely holds his ground against the ceaseless urging that he make light of sin and give himself up to the enjoyment of what is forbidden.

How consoling the knowledge and appreciation of this important truth must be to all who are firmly resolved to make the practice of perfect love of God the great purpose of their life on earth! What a brilliant crown of everlasting glory their heavenly Father is preparing for them in His eternal kingdom! "You are they who have continued with me in my temptations; and I dispose to you, as my Father hath disposed to me, a kingdom; that you may eat and drink at my table, in my kingdom, and may sit upon thrones, judging the twelve tribes of Israel."[28]

But there is another reason temptations help wonderfully to increase the love of God in the soul. It is found in the practice of frequent and fervent prayer to which they compel us to have recourse. How many ardent aspirations and earnest pleas for help are sent up to Heaven in the course of a single day by a soul harassed with temptations — prayers that probably would not be offered up if that soul were enjoying undisturbed peace and tranquillity! And how many acts of contrition will be made to atone for the partial yielding that may occur now and then, or because it is doubtful if the resistance offered to the temptation was strong enough to exclude even the smallest degree of sin! These prayers and acts of sorrow nourish the love of God in a wonderful way.

[28]Luke 22:28-30.

Temptations can help increase your merit and eternal glory

It must appear rather strange to uninstructed persons that St. James should write about temptations in this strain: "Brethren, count it all joy when you shall fall into diverse temptations"; and, "Blessed is the man that endureth temptation."[29]

Why should it be a source of joy to be tempted? And why is a man to consider himself blessed because he is tried by temptations?

St. James gives the answer: "For when he hath been proved, he shall receive the crown of life which God hath promised to them that love Him."[30]

That the patient endurance of temptations is a means of acquiring a wonderful growth of grace and merit here, and a corresponding degree of heavenly glory hereafter, is but a natural conclusion from what has been explained about growth of the love of God. Whatever contributes to the growth of this love — or of grace — also contributes to the growth of reward in Heaven.

[29]James 1:2, 12.

[30]James 1:12.

To make this point as clear as possible, let us contrast the spiritual life of two persons equally determined to serve God faithfully, of whom one is relatively free from temptations, while the other is almost continually assailed by them in a great variety of ways.

That which ordinarily proves to be the source of violent temptations for many others may be for one man not a temptation at all. He seems to be made of other material than his fellowmen. To some he may appear to be an angel in human flesh; to others he may seem to be lacking in certain human characteristics. Be this as it may. We suppose he is firmly resolved to avoid all sin and lead a life directed by love of God. Accordingly he is fervent in prayer, patient in suffering, full of charity to his neighbor and diligent in doing works of mercy. With the grace of God, he perseveres to the end. A rich reward is awaiting him in eternity.

The other, too, has resolved to practice the love of God in the highest degree of perfection. However, the conditions under which he is able to carry out his resolution differ completely. Perhaps by reason of early contact with sin — with or without his fault — or because of inherited tendencies or present unfavorable surroundings, he is subjected to countless temptations against the virtue of purity. They do not diminish with advancing years; rather, they grow more numerous. Although he is trying hard to lead a life of holiness, they do not cease to assail him; nay, it often seems that the more determined he is to serve God faithfully, the more do they pursue and torment him. Day after day he feels keenly the "sting of the flesh," and the "angel of Satan buffeting him";[31] the things that he sees, hears, and reads set up trains of thoughts, desires, and images of evil; he is often haunted by all kinds of unholy and foul suggestions; he frequently feels in his body the promptings of passion — in one word, his whole life is a ceaseless warfare against the whole host of temptations against purity.

Thus he finds himself in a very trying position, from which he is longing to be delivered. With St. Paul he often prays that the angel of Satan that is tormenting him may depart from him; but the answer that he receives is that which was given to St. Paul: "My grace is sufficient for thee; for power is made perfect in infirmity."[32]

Let the reader decide which of these two men is practicing a more perfect and more heroic love of God, and

[31] Cf. 2 Cor. 12:7.

[32] 2 Cor. 12:8-9.

hence acquiring more merit for Heaven. Surely there can be no doubt as to the answer. The love of the latter and the reward he is procuring for himself may exceed that of the former a hundred — nay, a thousandfold. Rightly considered, then, is it not a great advantage to be tried by the fiery ordeal of temptation rather than to enjoy calm and peace of soul, undisturbed by solicitations to sin and infidelity in the service of God?

What we have here explained in regard to temptations against the holy virtue of purity applies equally to all other kinds of temptation. Those who are molested with temptations of doubt in matters of faith; those who are troubled by distrust of God's goodness and mercy; those who are tempted to question God's justice and love in times of sickness, business reverses, persecutions, and other temporal calamities; those who are tormented by thoughts of blasphemy against God and the saints; those who are haunted by obscene fancies and images regarding even the most sacred objects, such as the crucifix, pictures, and statues of the saints; those who are assailed by strong impulses to take revenge in one form or another on an enemy; those who have to battle with thoughts of pride, vanity, self-complacency, and contempt of others — in one word, all who are tempted in any way whatsoever, should endeavor to console themselves by remembering that they are fighting the battles of the Lord and that, if they persevere to the end, the crown of eternal life will be awarded to them on their arrival at the portals of Heaven.

Thus we see how Divine Wisdom, which made use of the malice of some men against our Lord to bring about the redemption of man from the slavery of Satan, makes use of the ordeal of temptations to promote the spiritual and eternal interests of His devoted servants. The very means that Satan employs for the ruin of souls are converted into means of grace and merit. The truth that St. Paul teaches when he says, "To them that love God, all things work together unto good,"[33] extends also to the trials arising from our various temptations.

[33] Rom. 8:28.

Chapter Six

Deal prudently with temptations

The next point to be explained is how we should conduct ourselves during temptations. There are unhappily many persons who are disturbed and worried by the fear that they are remiss and negligent in resisting temptations; that they do not oppose them with sufficient strength of will; and that they are for this reason continually rendering themselves guilty of sin. This interferes with their spiritual life and, in particular, may easily keep them from receiving Holy Communion frequently or, when they do receive it, may make them unhappy with the fear that they are receiving it unworthily.

The following rules of conduct will prove helpful.

Be firm, but calm

The first requisite for success in your battle with temptations is *firmness of will* joined with *calmness of mind*.

How to Resist Temptation

The part that the will plays in the struggle with temptations was explained at length in the first chapter. It was stated there that the will is the sovereign that reigns over and dominates the soul's activity. Every human act — good as well as bad — is completed only when the will gives its consent. This is an interior, invisible action.

Hence, as any sin, no matter what its name, is committed, not at the moment when an outward act makes it visible to men (as, for example, theft, murder, or adultery), but at the moment when the will gives its consent and approval unseen by men (and this may be days and weeks before the outward act is attempted); so also is every resistance to a temptation an invisible act of the will, unseen by men, but clearly seen by the eye of God. Every act of virtue (as resistance to temptations always is) is therefore an interior and invisible act of the will, just as every sin is also such an act.

Hence, as long as the will, aided by the grace of God, maintains its attitude of firmness, there is no reason whatsoever to fear that a sin has been committed, even though the temptation may last a long time and may fill the mind with all kinds of evil thoughts and filthy pictures.

Firmness of will, then, is very necessary, but it is not enough. It is also necessary that you try to remain calm, self-controlled, composed in mind and body. Above all, guard against making use of nervous outward actions and gestures for the purpose of manifesting your interior resistance.

This last is a very important rule. There are some persons, especially those who are troubled with impure temptations and those who are scrupulous, who seem to think that it is necessary that they indicate their inward resolution by means of exterior acts and signs, such as the shaking of the head, the rolling of the eyes, jerky movements of the hands, audible words, and the like, all for the purpose of showing that they are offering resistance to their temptations.

All such exterior actions are not only not necessary, but even dangerous and harmful, and this for several reasons. First, in times of long-continued temptation, they produce fatigue of mind and body. Second, they make the person indulging in them restless, so that he becomes a source of distraction and distress to those around him. Third, they tend to make temptations more violent and insistent, since they rouse the nervous system (which is always affected by whatever troubles the soul). Finally, they provide the Devil with opportunities to add to the violence of the temptation.[34]

Let us explain this last statement. Although he knows a great deal about the mysterious workings of the human soul, the Devil does not know everything; but he is able to judge what is going on in its interior with a fair degree of accuracy. In forming these judgments he is guided by a person's outward actions, owing to the intimate connection existing between the soul and body. Thus, when a person exhibits an exterior restlessness in time of temptation and employs bodily movements to express his resistance, Satan can easily surmise what is going on in that person's soul. He can then work on the senses for the purpose of intensifying the temptation.

Hence, those who are tempted should above all see to it that they maintain an interior calmness of mind as well as an exterior calmness of body. This, together with firmness and determination of will, makes the struggle against temptation much easier. A right understanding of the fact that sin hinges on the will, and not on the feelings the temptations may produce, should contribute much toward maintaining that composure of soul

[34] See Chapter 3.

and body which is so helpful in our struggle with evil suggestions.

Do not fear temptations too much

In the next place, you must learn not to fear your temptations too much. Some persons are possessed with this fear. They are continually in a state of disquietude and unhappiness because they are afraid that they will be tempted. They are expecting to meet temptations everywhere, very much like timid persons who are afraid of encountering ghosts whenever they venture alone into dark places. Quite naturally, such an unreasonable fear of temptations causes undue thought about them. And this, in turn, easily leads to their actually springing up in the soul and giving rise to very severe conflicts.

While it is true that you must always have a wholesome fear of temptations, and never voluntarily cause them or rashly expose yourself to them, it is also true that you must cultivate a certain fearlessness and courage if you are to be victorious over temptations that you cannot escape. Learn to despise them and treat them with contempt. Refuse to argue or debate with them, and resolutely ignore their unholy suggestions.

St. Augustine[35] uses a very instructive example to show how we should meet our temptations. He compares the Devil — the author of many of our temptations — to a fierce dog that is securely tied with a strong chain. Such a beast can bark furiously and frighten timid persons by his barking; but he can injure only those who foolishly approach too closely. In the same way, Satan can solicit with his temptations, but he cannot force anyone to consent to them. He can cause us a great deal of distress and pain, but beyond that he can do us no harm.

A certain fearlessness is therefore a valuable asset in the battle that must be waged against temptations all through life. Success and victory favor the brave.

Offer indirect resistance

In the third place, try to resist your temptations indirectly rather than directly. Indirect resistance consists in this: when an evil thought, unholy desire, or impure sensation takes hold of you, do not attempt to dislodge, suppress, or remove it by a direct effort, or by wrestling

[35] St. Augustine (354-430), Bishop of Hippo.

with it, as it were. You cannot chase away an evil thought as you can drive away a dog with a stick, or cast an evil desire out of your mind as you can throw a book out the window, or get rid of an impure feeling as you can of a shoe that pinches you. As a rule, all such efforts to "get rid of" and to "drive away" a temptation will serve only to fix your attention still more on it and thus expose you to a greater conflict and to greater danger of consent.

What, then, is the better way? At the first approach of a temptation, try to brace yourself calmly but firmly for the conflict. Do not get excited, but make use of some fervent aspiration or short prayer addressed either to God directly, to the Blessed Virgin Mary, to your guardian angel, etc.; or you may make an agreement with God that a look at the crucifix or some similar act of devotion is to be an expression of the resistance of your will. Then, without deigning to argue with the temptation, or giving it any attention, try to apply your mind to some other affair and occupy yourself with that. This may be anything you can conveniently take up, e.g., conversation, reading, writing, manual labor, play, etc. If you can succeed in giving yourself up to some other thought or activity, you will find as a rule that the temptation will more easily lose its hold on you and depart.

If however, in spite of your efforts, your temptation should still continue, or return at frequent intervals, do not worry. Your will is remaining set against it, and that keeps you from giving consent. Fervently repeat your aspiration now and then, and try quietly to continue the work you may have in hand. Maintain your peace of soul by recalling that the mere feelings of pleasure and delight that go with the temptation do not of themselves constitute a sin, as was fully explained in the first part of this book. You can be confident that, with the help of divine grace, you will come out of the conflict victorious; and that, besides having given another proof of your true love of God, you will have acquired new claims to an eternal reward.

A very great help in our warfare against temptations is found in the cultivation of elevating and ennobling thoughts, especially such as are of a religious character. One who has mastered this secret will find that evil thoughts have far less power to force an entrance into his mind.

It is the idle, flighty, and trifling mind that easily becomes a roosting place for all kinds of sinful suggestions, imaginations, and thoughts. An idle mind is truly the Devil's workshop. "Idleness hath taught much evil."[36]

One, therefore, who is in earnest about loving God and keeping free from sin will endeavor at all times to occupy himself with thoughts that tend to raise his soul to higher things. For this purpose, he will make it a practice, as much as his business or work will allow, to read good books, especially such as treat of religious topics, and to avoid as useless and dangerous the ephemeral and trashy productions of the day. He realizes that the mind is like a mill. The millstones cannot turn out good flour if the grain that is poured on them is moldy and mildewed; likewise, the mind cannot be filled with good thoughts if it is fed with reading matter that is bound to suggest evil in one way or another. The same applies to conversations and to suggestive movies and theatrical productions.

The diligent practice of religious and spiritual reading cannot be recommended too earnestly, especially in these days, when every imaginable form of amusement and pleasure is at hand to make the soul all but totally forgetful of the awful realities of the life to come.

[36]Ecclus. 33:29 (RSV = Sir. 33:27).

Make your temptations known to your confessor

Another great help in the struggle against temptations is derived from making them known to our confessor or spiritual director. It is a very common experience that thereby they are considerably lessened and sometimes made to disappear altogether; indeed, even the mere resolution to make them known may produce this result.

There is no rule or law compelling us to tell our temptations in Confession; and, as was stated before, mere temptations are not to be confessed as sins. But the declaration of temptations is an act of humility sometimes far more difficult than the telling of even very serious sins. And it would seem that God is pleased at times to bestow an immediate reward for such humility, by granting a prompt removal of the temptation thus made known.

Besides, such an act of humility confounds and disarms Satan. Since he is an angel of darkness and therefore hates the light, he fears nothing so much as to see himself and his evil designs revealed. When, in time of temptation, a soul makes its condition known to God's representative, Satan's plans are crossed and frustrated. Hence, it is not at all surprising to find that he ceases, for a time at least, to molest the soul with his unholy suggestions.

In your struggle with temptations, it is a very good thing now and then to seek the advice of your confessor or the guide of your soul, and humbly follow his directions. God will not fail to reward your humility and obedience; and although He may not always remove the temptations, He will invariably grant you all the graces you need to keep you from falling into sin.

Pray and receive the sacraments

Finally, it is essential for success in this spiritual warfare that you make a proper and diligent use of prayer and the sacraments. So necessary are these two means that, without them, no hope of victory can ever be entertained. He who neglects them is foredoomed to defeat. His temptations will cast him down and subject him to the power of Satan.

Ever since human nature became infected with the poison of Original Sin, it has been impossible for man by himself to withstand the onslaught of the various temptations that beset him on all sides. It is only with the aid of God's supernatural grace that he can do this. But God has decreed that He will give His special graces only to those who have humility enough to ask for them in prayer. Hence there is no hope of safety from sin for him who fails for any reason to implore God for these graces by frequent and earnest pleadings. On the other hand, he who has recourse to Him by fervent prayer in times of temptation is sure to experience the truth of our Lord's promise that whatever we pray for with confidence will be granted to us.

But it is especially in the sacraments that God has provided powerful aids for us in our struggle against sin and temptation. Hence, those who are truly in earnest about overcoming all their temptations will diligently avail themselves of these aids. There are two sacraments in particular that have been instituted for this purpose — namely, those of *Penance* and the *Holy Eucharist*. The frequent and fervent reception of these, together with the earnest endeavor to use to the best advantage the graces they impart, cannot but lead to victory over the suggestions of evil that we continually encounter from the enemies of our soul: the world, the flesh, and the Devil.

If, happily, you are so situated as to be able to receive Holy Communion frequently, perhaps even daily, do not fail to make a good use of this opportunity, for two reasons: first, to enrich yourself daily more and more with the wonderful graces of this greatest of the Seven Sacraments, and thereby to increase your treasure of heavenly merits in a most remarkable way; and second, to fortify yourself daily for the conflict you must wage with your spiritual enemies. Do not make the fatal mistake that many uninstructed persons fall into: of remaining away from Holy Communion because you are tempted, thus depriving yourself of its powerful help just when you need it most. Do not forget that this sacrament is meant to be, among other things, a medicine that gives you power and strength to resist the assaults of Satan successfully. When you are tempted, therefore, try to receive Holy Communion all the more eagerly. Does a sensible man refuse to take medicine on the plea that he is sick?

God, who knows perfectly the many needs of the human soul in its struggle for holiness and purity, has provided a bountiful and effective remedy in the graces of the sacraments. But keep in mind one important truth: these sacraments do not dispense with your faithful cooperation. You must use your willpower. Without that, even the most powerful graces will be of no avail. Grace will not free you from temptations, but it will help you to resist them and not do their bidding. Resistance to temptations is to be *your* work; it is to be one of your means of winning Heaven. "My grace is sufficient for thee" was the answer St. Paul received when he prayed for deliverance from his temptation.[37]

The faithful use of the several means here explained will make it possible for you to win the victory over all the temptations to which you may be exposed in the course of your life.

True, these means will not do away with your temptations, but they will enable you to hold out against them, so that you will not consent to them and thus render yourself guilty of sin. It will be far more glorious for you in the end to have been severely tried by temptations, under which you proved your love of God by manfully resisting, than to have enjoyed the privilege of complete exemption from them. Freedom from them would indeed render your life peaceful and pleasant, but it would also deprive you of countless opportunities to

[37] 2 Cor. 12:9.

prove your love of God and to increase your future glory in Heaven.

Take heart, therefore, and resolve courageously to resist all your temptations with implicit reliance on God's grace, fully assured that "he that shall have overcome shall receive the crown of life which God hath promised to them that love Him."[38]

[38]Cf. James 1:12.

Chapter Seven

Learn from others' example

Having explained in the preceding chapters the various aspects of the subject of temptations, we will in this concluding chapter place before you a few examples taken from the lives of the saints to illustrate and confirm what has been set forth.

Temptations can demonstrate your love for God

Our first example, the elder Tobias, is taken from the Old Testament. Humanly speaking — that is, according to the standards of those not enlightened by the Christian Faith — it must be said that if ever there was a man who had reason to call in question the justice of God and to deny His goodness, it was this saintly man.

Although from his earliest youth he had carefully avoided sin and led a life of virtue and holiness, he was made to suffer with the rest of his fellow countrymen all the trials and hardships of the Babylonian captivity.

We can easily surmise that under this trial, he must have been assailed by the temptation to find fault with the ways of God and to murmur against His holy will. Why should he, although innocent, be made to suffer with his fellows who were being punished for their sin of idolatry? But he firmly resisted this temptation. He refused to investigate the unsearchable dispensations of Divine Providence and to murmur against His ordinances. On the contrary, he submitted with admirable resignation to the divine will and humbly endured the evils that his nation was made to suffer for its sins of apostasy and idol worship.

Nor was this all. Another and still more painful trial was in store for him. "Now, it happened one day," we read in the book of Tobias, "that being wearied with burying [the dead], he came to his house and cast himself down by the wall and slept. And as he was sleeping, hot dung out of a swallow's nest fell upon his eyes, and he was made blind. Now, this trial, therefore, the Lord permitted to happen to him that an example might be given to posterity of his patience, as also of holy Job. For whereas he had always feared God from his infancy and kept His commandments, he repined not against God because the evil of blindness had befallen him, but continued immovable in the fear of God, giving thanks to God all the days of his life."[39]

Thus we see how this great affliction, far from causing Tobias to sin against God by murmuring and calling His justice in question, served only to strengthen further his faith and trust in Him. We can hardly conceive that the temptation to find fault with God's dealings toward him did not make violent assaults on his soul. But his faith and trust were solid and strong. And for this he merited the favor of a perfect cure and the consoling assurance from the archangel Raphael: "Because thou wast acceptable to God, it was necessary that temptation should prove thee."[40]

Even great saints experience temptations

We cannot read the letters of St. Paul, the great Apostle of the Gentiles, without deriving therefrom the

[39]Tob. 2:10-14.

[40]Tob. 12:13.

benefit of valuable instructions regarding temptation. It will therefore be very helpful to consider a few passages in which this subject is touched on.

That we must all through life struggle against all kinds of temptations is emphasized by St. Paul in many places, and these reveal what he himself was made to endure from them. He speaks of the ceaseless warfare that must be waged between the man of sin and the man of grace; between the natural and the supernatural man. Thus he says, "I am delighted with the law of God, according to the inward man [i.e., enlightened by grace]; but I see another law in my members fighting against the law of my mind, and captivating me in the law of sin that is in my members [i.e., the inclination to sin that is in me by reason of the poison of Original Sin]. Unhappy man that I am; who shall deliver me from the body of this death?"[41]

That he finds the doing of evil easy and natural, while the doing of good requires vigorous action on the part of the will strengthened by divine grace, he tells in the following words: "To will [good] is present with me [i.e., I desire to do good]; but to accomplish that which

[41] Rom. 7:22-24.

is good I find not. For the good which I will, I do not; but the evil which I will not, that I do. . . . I find, then, a law, that when I have a will to do good, evil is present with me."[42]

In his letter to the Galatians he again points out this opposition between the natural and the supernatural: "Walk in the spirit, and you shall not fulfill the lusts of the flesh. For the flesh lusteth against the spirit, and the spirit against the flesh; for these are contrary one to another, so that you do not the things that you would."[43]

How, despite his great holiness and high rank as an apostle, St. Paul was subjected, in God's dispensation, to what seem to have been violent assaults on his chastity can be gathered from the following passages: "Lest the greatness of the revelations should exalt me [make me proud], there was given me a sting of my flesh, an angel of Satan to buffet me. For which thing I thrice besought the Lord that it might depart from me. And He said to me: My grace is sufficient for thee; for power [virtue] is made perfect in infirmity."[44]

[42]Rom. 7:18, 19, 21.

[43]Gal. 5:16-17.

[44]2 Cor. 12:7-9.

Many other passages could be cited, but these few will suffice to prove that great holiness is compatible with many and severe temptations; that even so great a saint as St. Paul was subjected to them; and that, with the all-powerful help of God's grace, every man is able, despite his inherent weakness and proneness to sin, to be at all times victorious over his temptations, whether they spring from his own rebellious passions or from the malice of Satan. "My grace is sufficient for thee."

Temptations can serve as penance for past sins

That temptations are meant to be utilized as a means of doing penance and making atonement for our past sins, as also for the acquisition of a high degree of holiness, is well illustrated in the life of St. Mary of Egypt, who died about the year 421.

This holy penitent had the misfortune of having, in her early youth, embraced a life of sin, in which she spent no fewer than seventeen years. When at last she was converted by a special grace obtained through the intercession of the Blessed Virgin Mary, she resolved to spend the rest of her life in the practice of severe penance for the purpose of expiating her wicked deeds. Leaving her home, she took up her abode in a desert, where she spent about forty-seven years in rigorous penitential works.

For seventeen years after her conversion, she was sorely tried and afflicted by all kinds of temptations. It would seem as if God desired for her to spend as many years in doing penance by wrestling with Satan and her own evil inclinations as she had spent in sinful living and, by this means, to make a painful atonement for the sins she had committed and the scandal she had given. Let us hear her telling it in her own words:

> Seventeen years I spent in the most violent temptations and almost perpetual conflicts with my inordinate desires. I was tempted to regret the flesh and fish of Egypt and the wines that I drank in the world to excess, whereas here I often could not come by a drop of water to quench my thirst. Other desires made assaults on my mind; but weeping and striking my breast on those occasions, I called to mind the vows I had made under the protection of the Blessed Virgin and begged her to obtain my deliverance from the affliction

> and dangers of such thoughts. After long weeping and bruising my body with blows, I found myself suddenly enlightened and my mind restored to a perfect calm. Often the tyranny of my old passions seemed ready to drag me out of the desert; at those times, I threw myself on the ground and watered it with my tears, raising my heart continually to the Blessed Virgin until she procured me comfort; and she never failed to show herself my faithful Protectress.

Thus, we can learn from the example and experience of this holy penitent that temptations, even those which have their origin in our own past sins, can be converted, by the grace of God, into means of complete expiation for these violations of God's holy law, as also into means of heroic virtue and of a wonderful increase of grace here and glory hereafter.

Temptations can increase merit and heavenly glory

At times God allows His chosen friends, even those who have never lost their baptismal innocence, to be assailed by very violent and humiliating temptations, in order to test their virtue and give them opportunities for gaining a large increase of grace and merit. We learn this from the life of St. Catherine of Siena.

St. Catherine was born in 1347. From her earliest infancy, her heart was turned to God, and she was remarkable for her love of mortification and prayer. Even in her childhood, she consecrated her virginity to God by a private vow. This brought on her a great deal of suffering. Her parents insisted that she enter the married state, but she resolutely refused to change her determination to lead the life of virginity. To break her will, they subjected her to harsh treatment and made her do all the drudgery of the house. But nothing could force her to change her resolution. At the age of eighteen, she joined the Third Order of St. Dominic.

But what we desire to bring particularly to your attention is the conflict that this saint was made to undergo with temptations of the most violent kind. Satan set all his engines to work for an assault on her virtue. He first filled her imagination with the most filthy representations and assailed her heart with the basest and most humbling temptations. After this he spread in her soul such a cloud of darkness that it was a trial unimaginably severe. She saw herself a hundred times on the brink of the precipice, but was always supported by an invisible hand. Her means of defense were fervent prayer, humility, resignation, and confidence in God. By these she persevered and was at last delivered from her trials, which had served only to purify her heart more fully from the stains of human imperfection.

Our divine Savior was pleased to appear to her after the conflict was over. "Where wast Thou!" she complainingly said to Him, "whilst I was in such an abandoned and frightful condition?" "I was with thee," He replied. "What?" she said. "In the midst of all the filthy abominations with which my heart was infested?" He replied, "They were displeasing and most painful to thee. This conflict, therefore, was thy merit, and thy victory over them was owing to my presence."

This is but another proof of the truth that, for God's faithful servants, temptations are not occasions of sin, but means of solid virtue, of rapid growth in grace, and of great increase of heavenly merit.

Temptations can draw you closer to God

St. Mary Magdalen de Pazzi furnishes an instructive example of the truth that the highest degree of holiness and union with God is attained only through painful trials of soul and body.

We must always keep in mind that God demands from His true servants that they seek Him alone, and with great purity of intention, and that they detach their hearts from all earthly pleasures. Wherefore, to free them perfectly from all secret self-love, that they may be fitted to become vessels of His pure love, He casts them into the crucible of interior tribulation; and usually the higher the degree of sanctity to which, in His mercy, He deigns to raise them, the more severe the fire is.

Our saint experienced this by the state of interior desolation into which she fell from a state of great interior joy after her consecration to God in the religious life. But she came out of this ordeal with great spiritual gain; her virtue was solid because it was humble, patient, and constant. She did not desire heavenly consolations, deeming herself the most unworthy of all God's creatures; and the favors she received she endeavored to conceal from others, referring them entirely to the gratuitous goodness of God.

To advance her to a very high degree of holiness, our Lord gave her to understand that she must pass through an extremely severe ordeal of temptations of various kinds, and a state of great suffering that she describes as "the lions' den." For the space of five years, she suffered, in addition to bodily ailments, the most grievous and violent temptations to impurity, gluttony, pride, infidelity, and blasphemy. Her imagination was often filled with those abominations whose very name fills chaste souls with horror.

Her mind was troubled with the most hideous images of hellish monsters, and like Job, she seemed abandoned to the powers of Hell. Her soul was plunged into a state of darkness in which she was able to discern nothing but horror in herself and in all things about her. Thoughts of blasphemy and infidelity tormented her so violently that she sometimes cried out to her sisters, "Pray for me that I may not blaspheme God instead of praising Him." This condition of intense suffering lasted no fewer than five years, when, on the feast of Pentecost 1590, she was suddenly freed from it, and great peace of soul was granted to her. Her death occurred on May 25, 1607.

Truly this is a convincing illustration that "virtue is made perfect in infirmity,"[45] and that even in the midst

[45]Cf. 2 Cor. 12:9.

of the most severe temptations, a soul solidly established in the grace and love of God can advance by leaps and bounds on the way to Christian perfection.

The saints show you how to resist temptation

In placing before you the example of St. Vincent de Paul (c. 1580-1660), we desire to point out how those who are tormented by temptations should conduct themselves in order to resist them successfully, and not be unduly disturbed by them.

The particular temptation by which St. Vincent found himself severely tried was that of doubt in matters of faith. It came about in this way.

There lived at that time a priest, a doctor of theology, who was very severely troubled with this temptation of doubt — so much so that his health began to fail, and he was on the verge of despair. St. Vincent was deeply afflicted at seeing his friend in this pitiable condition. He feared lest his lips should at length open to blasphemy and his heart to irreligion. To obtain the mercy of God, who punished so rigorously the idleness, and perhaps also the self-complacency, to which the doctor had too much yielded, St. Vincent had recourse to prayer. Imitating in some degree the charity of our Savior, who took upon Himself our weaknesses to heal them, he offered himself to God as a victim. In order to satisfy the Divine Justice, he consented himself to bear either that species of trial or any other punishment which God would be pleased to inflict.

So earnest and so fervent a prayer, which very closely resembled the desire of St. Paul to be anathema for his brethren,[46] was heard in its whole extent. The sick man was entirely delivered from his temptations. A profound peace succeeded the storm. The cloud that had obscured his faith was dispersed. His love for Jesus Christ was more tender than ever, and until the day of his death, he blessed God for having proportioned the consolation to His past rigor.

But the temptation of the theologian passed into the soul of Vincent as rapidly as the leprosy of Naaman attacked Giezi.[47] The first impressions of an evil, which is never felt so much as when we are personally assailed by it, appeared to astonish him. The new Job seemed to be a prey to all the furies of the Devil; but far from losing

[46] Cf. Rom. 9:3.

[47] Cf. 4 Kings 5:20-27 (RSV = 2 Kings 5:20-27).

courage, he knew how to make them useful. For that purpose, he made it a law always to act in opposition to what was suggested to him by the seducer.

One of the means he made use of in this conflict was the following: he wrote out the Apostles' Creed on a piece of paper, which he carried folded over his heart. He also made an agreement with God that as often as he placed his hand over this written profession of Faith, it was meant to be an act of faith in opposition to the temptation that was assailing him. This was a very simple but very effective remedy. Whenever he was troubled by a temptation, he calmly placed his hand over his heart and quietly continued to do whatever work he had in hand. He refused to argue or dispute with the evil thought. If the temptation did not cease, or if it returned, he simply repeated this action every now and then without allowing himself to be troubled about the possibility of having given consent to the thought.

He groaned under the weight of this severe trial during the space of four whole years, all the while remaining faithful in his service of God. He continued to render to our Lord all the honor he was capable of and especially served Him in the hospitals, in the persons of the poor, with a most zealous fervor.

At last God was pleased to restore peace to his soul. This favor was the reward of a new effort of charity, which consisted in his taking a firm and inviolable resolution to consecrate all his life to the service of the afflicted. Scarcely had he taken this resolution when the temptation vanished and his heart tasted a sweet and perfect liberty.

Temptations can help you rely on God

We introduce St. John Vianney (1786-1859), the holy Curé of Ars, to illustrate what our conduct should be when we are afflicted with dryness, or aridity, or even a positive disgust for prayer and the service of God. What is commonly known as spiritual dryness can very properly be called a temptation, inasmuch as it is for weak souls an occasion of discouragement and hence often of complete abandonment of the spiritual life.

Thus we read in his life: As if to increase his merit and to render his zeal more disinterested, our Lord had drawn a veil before his eyes in such a way that he did not perceive the immense amount of good that was being effected through his agency. He thought himself a useless person, without faith, intelligence, discernment, or virtue; fit only to ruin everything, to disedify everyone, to be an obstacle to all good.

The humility of his heart caused him to shed very real tears over his shortcomings, his want of devotion, his ignorance; and his grief could be stemmed only by the generosity of a courage which urged him to cast himself headlong, with all his incapacities, into the arms of our Lord.

"God," said he, "has done me this great mercy, that He has given me nothing on which I can lean — neither talents, wisdom, knowledge, strength, nor virtue. When I enter into myself, I can discover nothing but my poor sins. Nevertheless the good God permits it that I do not see them all and that I do not know myself completely. That spectacle would cause me to despair. Against this temptation to despair I have only one resource: to throw myself at the foot of the tabernacle like a little dog at the feet of his master."

An important lesson that is to be learned from the example of this holy priest is a persevering trust in God in times of temptation, especially temptation against faith and hope, and an unswerving fidelity to our duties and spiritual exercises. This it is that wins for the soul God's special favors, since it is during such trials that the soul exhibits the most solid proofs of true love of Him and is at the same time placed in a position of making vast gains in grace and merit.

Christ Himself shows you how to resist temptations

Finally, we have the example furnished us by none other than the Saint of Saints, our blessed Savior, Jesus Christ. There is very much to be learned from this for our instruction and consolation.

There were three distinct kinds of temptation by which our divine Savior allowed Lucifer to assail Him. These correspond to the three great lusts, as St. John calls them, that are the root causes of all our temptations and sins. The first was that of sensual pleasure, in the form of gluttony.[48] The second was that of vainglory and pride, as suggested by the words of the tempter: "If Thou be the Son of God, cast Thyself down. . . ."[49] The third was that of avarice and ambition, the Devil falsely promising our Lord the dominion of all the kingdoms of

[48] Cf. Matt. 4:3.

[49] Matt. 4:6.

the world: "All these things I will give Thee, if falling down, Thou wilt adore me."[50]

These temptations of our Lord are at once our consolation, our strength, and our instruction. They are our consolation, because they comfort us when we are undergoing similar interior trials, knowing that He also allowed Himself to experience suggestions of evil by the enemy of God and man.

They are our strength, because He has won for us, and placed at our disposal, all the graces we need to resist our temptations successfully; and not only this, but because they also become for us occasions of rich merit.

Finally, they are our instruction, because our Lord teaches us by His example how to contend with our temptations calmly and confidently, resting on our faith and trusting in God. He teaches us not to argue with the tempter and his foul suggestions, but peremptorily to declare ourselves for the will and law of God. His use of Sacred Scripture teaches us how we must combat our temptations with the thoughts and truths of Faith, thus employing, as St. Paul calls it, "the shield of Faith

[50] Matt. 4:9.

wherewith to extinguish the fiery darts of the most wicked one."[51]

Thus was our divine Savior pleased to give us a practical lesson in the manner in which we must wage our warfare against the many temptations that come to us as the sad legacy of Original Sin. The very fact that He, the All-Holy, who cannot endure sin, but must by His very nature hate it with an infinite and eternal hatred, permitted Satan to approach Him with suggestions of sin, shows us that there is no sin in being tempted; that even the holiest persons must expect to undergo this trial; and that temptations are intimately bound up with the process of sanctification, by which our souls are to be fitted to become partakers of that eternal glory which the Son of God procured for us by the humiliations and sufferings He endured in His human nature.

Take courage, then, dear reader, and struggle manfully against an evil to which your divine Savior submitted for your consolation and instruction. Hear Him encourage you: "Fear not; I have overcome the world."[52] And never lose sight of His gracious promise: "You are

[51] Cf. Eph. 6:16.

[52] Cf. John 16:33.

they who have continued with me in my temptations; and I dispose to you, as my Father hath disposed to me, a kingdom: that you may eat and drink at my table, in my kingdom, and may sit upon thrones, judging the twelve tribes of Israel."[53]

[53] Luke 22:28-30.

Biographical Note

Francis J. Remler

(1874-1962)

Born in Bavaria in Germany, Francis Remler moved to the United States at the age of fourteen. He graduated from St. Benedict's College in Atchinson, Kansas, in 1895 and the following year entered the Vincentian seminary in Perryville, Missouri. He taught German briefly at St. Vincent's College (now De Paul University), of which he was a member of the pioneer faculty, and was ordained to the priesthood in 1902.

Fr. Remler spent many years serving at Kenrick Seminary, teaching German, literature, homiletics, and science, and serving as assistant director of seminarians, procurator of the seminary, and spiritual director.

In 1940, Fr. Remler entered semi-retirement, but even that kept him busy giving numerous retreats, preparing a Layman's Home Retreat with a fellow priest, and writing many pamphlets and books, including *How to Resist Temptation*, *The Eternal Inheritance*, and *Why*

How to Resist Temptation

Must I Suffer? Drawing on the example and inspiration of Christ and the saints, Fr. Remler's writings continue to offer today's readers clear, simple explanations on the truths of the Faith that touch the lives of all Christians each day.

Sophia Institute Press®

Sophia Institute

Sophia Institute is a nonprofit institution that seeks to nurture the spiritual, moral, and cultural life of souls and to spread the Gospel of Christ in conformity with the authentic teachings of the Roman Catholic Church.

Sophia Institute Press fulfills this mission by offering translations, reprints, and new publications that afford readers a rich source of the enduring wisdom of mankind.

Sophia Institute also operates two popular online Catholic resources: CrisisMagazine.com and CatholicExchange.com.

Crisis Magazine provides insightful cultural analysis that arms readers with the arguments necessary for navigating the ideological and theological minefields of the day. *Catholic Exchange* provides world news from a Catholic perspective as well as daily devotionals and articles that will help you to grow in holiness and live a life consistent with the teachings of the Church.

In 2013, Sophia Institute launched Sophia Institute for Teachers to renew and rebuild Catholic culture through service to Catholic education. With the goal of nurturing the spiritual, moral, and cultural life of souls, and an abiding respect for the role and work of teachers, we strive to provide materials and programs that are at once enlightening to the mind and ennobling to the heart; faithful and complete, as well as useful and practical.

Sophia Institute gratefully recognizes the Solidarity Association for preserving and encouraging the growth of our apostolate over the course of many years. Without their generous and timely support, this book would not be in your hands.

www.SophiaInstitute.com
www.CatholicExchange.com
www.CrisisMagazine.com
www.SophiaInstituteforTeachers.org

Sophia Institute Press® is a registered trademark of Sophia Institute.
Sophia Institute is a tax-exempt institution as defined by the Internal Revenue Code, Section 501(c)(3). Tax I.D. 22-2548708.